高职高专"十二五"规划教材
21世纪高职高专能力本位型系列规划教材·市场营销系列

# 电子商务英语(第2版)

主　　编　陈晓鸣　　叶海鹏
副 主 编　魏振锋　　吴　适
参　　编　闫艳红　　朱飒飒　　戴凯西

北京大学出版社
PEKING UNIVERSITY PRESS

## 内容简介

本书根据电子商务专业的实际需要，结合贸易、计算机及信息技术等专业英语的相关内容编写而成，内容主要涉及网络购物、网店运营、网络沟通、网页制作、网络营销、网络支付、贸易术语、国际贸易等方面。全书贯彻"实时、实用、实际"的编写原则，重点突出"够用、能用、可用"的要求，力求将最常用的电子商务英语专业词汇及用法集中呈现给读者。

本书可作为高职高专电子商务专业的英语教材，也可作为从事电子商务行业人员的培训教材。

**图书在版编目(CIP)数据**

电子商务英语/陈晓鸣，叶海鹏主编．—2版．—北京：北京大学出版社，2014.8
(21世纪高职高专能力本位型系列规划教材·市场营销系列)
ISBN 978-7-301-24585-9

Ⅰ. ①电⋯ Ⅱ. ①陈⋯②叶⋯ Ⅲ. ①电子商务—英语—高等职业教育—教材 Ⅳ. ①H31

中国版本图书馆 CIP 数据核字(2014)第 176458 号

| | |
|---|---|
| 书　　　名： | 电子商务英语（第2版） |
| 著作责任者： | 陈晓鸣　叶海鹏　主编 |
| 策划编辑： | 蔡华兵 |
| 责任编辑： | 陈颖颖 |
| 标准书号： | ISBN 978-7-301-24585-9/F · 4005 |
| 出版发行： | 北京大学出版社 |
| 地　　　址： | 北京市海淀区成府路205号　100871 |
| 网　　　址： | http://www.pup.cn　新浪官方微博：@北京大学出版社 |
| 电子信箱： | pup_6@163.com |
| 电　　　话： | 邮购部 62752015　发行部 62750672　编辑部 62750667　出版部 62754962 |
| 印　　刷　者： | 北京鑫海金澳胶印有限公司 |
| 经　　销　者： | 新华书店 |
| | 787毫米×1092毫米　16开本　13.25印张　300千字 |
| | 2010年8月第1版 |
| | 2014年8月第2版　2018年8月第5次印刷（总第8次印刷） |
| 定　　　价： | 27.00元 |

未经许可，不得以任何方式复制或抄袭本书之部分或全部内容。
版权所有，侵权必究
举报电话：010-62752024　电子信箱：fd@pup.pku.edu.cn

# 第 2 版前言

随着我国电子商务的迅猛发展，电子商务已经在人们的社会生活中发挥了重要的作用。商务部预计到 2015 年，我国网络零售额将占到全社会消费品零售总额的 10%以上，我国规模以上企业（统计术语，一般以年产量作为企业规模的标准，国家对不同行为企业都制订了一个规模要求，达到规模要求的企业就称为规模以上企业）应用电子商务比例将达到 80%以上。现代电子商务起源于美国，一些最新的商业应用也大都源自国外，如社交网络、微博等，因此在电子商务的学习过程中，不可避免地需要借助英语来学习电子商务的历史、现状与发展趋势，以更好、更快、更全地学习专业知识、把握行业动态、适应企业需要，为将来的就业或创业活动打下良好的专业英语基础。

随着我国网络经济的深入发展，越来越多的企业需要吸收国外网络经济发展的经验与教训，所以电子商务专业学生借助电子商务英语学习国外网络经济发展与电子商务应用的需要尤为迫切。但目前一般的电子商务英语教材要么难度偏高（适合本科层次学生使用），要么难度偏低（适合中职层次学生使用），很难与高职高专层次学生的专业基础和英语水平相匹配。因此，编者结合自身多年教学经验，联合温州地区几所高职院校讲授电子商务英语的教师，编写了这本针对高职高专层次学生的教材。

---

## 关于本课程

电子商务英语是电子商务专业的专业英语课程，涉及市场营销、信息技术、国际贸易等领域的专业术语，具有较强的综合性，是计算机英语与商务英语等专业英语的交叉学科。近年来随着电子商务应用的不断扩大，其范畴还有进一步扩大的趋势，比如微博、微信等。

电子商务英语是高职高专电子商务专业的一门技能性课程，实用性和操作性较强，它主要通过专业英语工具学习把握国外电子商务的最新发展动态，为学生从事跨国电子商务打下外语基础。电子商务英语让学生通过一定的专业术语学习后，在专业教师的指导下，阅读一些英语原版电子商务资料，开拓学生视野，启发学生思想，在较短的时间内使学生初步具备使用英语学习电子商务的能力。

## 关于本书

本书以"实时、实用、实际"为原则，按照学生"够用、能用、可用"的要求来进行编写。2 版在内容上较 1 版进行了大量更新，尽可能采用最新数据（如 2013 "双十一"），尽可能介绍最新应用（如微信），力求将电子商务英语最新动态集中呈现给读者。由于高职高专电子商务专业的培养目标是将学生培养成从事一线电子商务操作的高技能人才，编者采用"虚拟人物"的方法，以一名高职院校电子商务专业学生"Lisa Lee"从网络购物者到网店经营者的身份转变为线索，将从事电子商务工作涉及的专业英语串联起来。此外，本书还参考国外相关教材的写法，从第一人称的角度将"最常见、最实用、最可用"的电子商务英语以叙事主题的形式逐一呈现，有助于提高学生的英语应用能力和从事相关工作的操作技能。

本书共分为 9 个单元，每个单元结合外语教材惯例与电商热门应用分为 4 个模块，即博客、精读、泛读与相关链接。博客模块主要介绍故事情节；精读模块主要介绍电商背景知识；泛读模块主要介绍电商拓展知识；相关链接模块主要介绍电商成功案例。书中相应部分还有注释、翻译贴士、练习，用以巩固所学内容、提升自学能力。

## 如何使用本书

本书内容按照 36～40 学时安排，推荐学时分配为每单元 4 学时。当然也可灵活安排学时，对某些单元进行增删讲解。博客与精读模块建议教师详细讲解，泛读与相关链接模块建议教师略作讲解或由学生自学。

## 本书编写队伍

本书由陈晓鸣（温州科技职业学院）、叶海鹏（温州科技职业学院）担任主编，由魏振锋（浙江工贸职业技术学院）、吴适（浙江工贸职业技术学院）担任副主编，闫艳红（浙江东方职业技术学院）、朱飒飒（温州科技职业学院）、戴凯西（温州科技职业学院）参加了编写。具体编写分工如下：Unit One，陈晓鸣、戴凯西；Unit Two，叶海鹏、朱飒飒；Unit Three，叶海鹏；Unit Four，魏振锋；Unit Five，吴适；Unit Six，闫艳红；Unit Seven，魏振锋；Unit Eight，陈晓鸣；Unit Nine，吴适。陈晓鸣负责本书的总体设计以及统稿工作。

本书在编写过程中，还参考和引用了国内外相关的文献资料，听取了有关人士的宝贵经验和建议，取长补短。在此谨向对本书编写、出版提供过帮助的人士表示衷心的感谢！

---

由于编者水平有限，编写时间仓促，书中难免存在不妥之处，敬请广大读者批评指正。您的宝贵意见请反馈到邮箱 sywat716@126.com。

编　者

2014 年 3 月

# 目 录

## Unit One  Wonderful Internet ... 1

- Blog: What Can I Do on the Internet? ... 3
- Intensive Reading: What a Wonderful Net! ... 8
- Extensive Reading: Shop and Brand ... 10
- Related Links: Alipay ... 12

## Unit Two  Online Shopping ... 19

- Blog: Shopping without Going Out! ... 21
- Intensive Reading: The Development of E-commerce ... 26
- Extensive Reading: Online Payment ... 29
- Related Links: McDonald's Goes Online to Sell Consumer Goods ... 31
- China Eastern Airlines and Alibaba Group Form Strategic Alliance in E-commerce ... 32

## Unit Three  Online Payment ... 41

- Blog: I Can Make It Now! ... 43
- Intensive Reading: Logistics ... 48
- Extensive Reading: International Trade through E-commerce ... 51
- Related Links: PayPal ... 53

## Unit Four  Web Design ... 59

- Blog: Learning Web Design ... 61
- Intensive Reading: The Structure of an HTML Page ... 68
- Extensive Reading: Web Layout Basics ... 72
- Related Links: Adobe ... 75

## Unit Five  Managing Online Business ... 83

- Blog: Open an E-shop ... 85
- Intensive Reading: Running a Business on the Internet ... 92
- Extensive Reading: Trends in Social Media Use in China ... 95
- Related Links: Popular Social Media Platforms ... 98

## Unit Six  E-marketing ... 105

- Blog: My E-marketing ... 107
- Intensive Reading: The Year 1997 and E-marketing ... 113
- Extensive Reading: Start Advertising with Search Engine ... 115
- Related Links: Selling on Amazon.com ... 117

## Unit Seven    Network Communication ·········· 127

Blog: Internet Communication ·········· 129
Intensive Reading: Microblogging ·········· 135
Extensive Reading: WeChat ·········· 139
Related Links: Facebook ·········· 142

## Unit Eight    Trade Terms ·········· 151

Blog: Price Terms ·········· 153
Intensive Reading: Why Prices Are So Different in International Trade? ·········· 159
Extensive Reading: Insurance ·········· 161
Related Links: Aliexpress, Escrow and Alipay ·········· 163

## Unit Nine    Global Trading ·········· 171

Blog: My Global Trading ·········· 173
Intensive Reading: Exploring Distribution Channel Online ·········· 181
Extensive Reading: China's E-Commerce Companies Go Global ·········· 184
Related Links: Alibaba.com ·········· 186

附录一　电子商务常用术语中英文对照表 ·········· 195

附录二　全球知名电子商务网站60例 ·········· 197

附录三　部分练习答案举例 ·········· 199

参考文献 ·········· 203

# Unit One
## Wonderful Internet

Blog: What Can I Do on the Internet?

Intensive Reading: What a Wonderful Net!

Extensive Reading: Shop and Brand

Related Links: Alipay

## What Can I Do on the Internet?

Hi! My name is **Lisa Lee** and I am 19 years old. I am a sophomore majoring in **E-commerce**, studying in a nice **vocational college** in Wenzhou, Zhejiang **Province**, **PRC**.

Today is Saturday, and it's raining **heavily**. **Originally**, I can go out to have a walk around the city because it's my holiday. If possible, I want to buy a book called **"Big Data: A Revolution That Will Transform How We Live, Work and Think"**. But I hate to go out while it's raining because it's very **inconvenient** for me to ride a bicycle or take a bus. Of course, to take a taxi is better, but it's too expensive for me to **afford**.

My parents are working very hard, they almost don't have any holidays. They are **businessmen** and they must **manage** their shop every day including weekends. They even think holidays are their **peak season** for business. So, they don't have time to be with me during weekends. Because of the heavy rain, a nice holiday is going to be a boring day!

I begin to think how to spend my holiday after 5 days' study. To review my lessons? No, at least not this morning! It's raining even more heavily outside, what can I do without going out? Oh, yes! Why not **surf** on the Internet?

[1] **Lisa Lee**：李丽莎
[2] **E-commerce**：电子商务
[3] **vocational college**：职业学院
[4] **Province**：[ˈprɔvins] *n.* 省
[5] **PRC**：中华人民共和国

[6] **heavily**：[ˈhevili] *adv.* 很重地
[7] **Originally**：[əˈridʒənəli] *adv.* 原本

[8] **Big Data: A Revolution That Will Transform How We Live, Work and Think**：《大数据时代：生活、工作与思想的大变革》

[9] **inconvenient**：[ˌinkənˈviːnjənt] *adj.* 不方便的

[10] **afford**：[əˈfɔːd] *v.* 负担得起

[11] **businessmen**：businessman [ˈbiznismæn] 的复数，*n.* 商人
[12] **manage**：[ˈmænidʒ] *v.* 经营，管理
[13] **peak season**：高峰期，旺季

[14] **surf**：[səːf] *v.* 冲浪

[1] **power button**：电源按钮
[2] **user name**：['ju:zə neim] *n.* 用户名
[3] **password**：['pɑ:swə:d] *n.* 密码，口令
[4] **logo**：['lɔgəu] *n.* 图标，标识
[5] **Microsoft**：['maikrəsɔft] *n.* 微软
[6] **Windows XP**：*n.* 最流行的一种计算机操作系统
[7] **Internet Explorer**：IE 浏览器
[8] **desktop**：['desktɔp] *n.* 桌面
[9] **click**：[klik] *v.* 点击
[10] **window** ['windəu] *n.* 窗口
[11] **popup**：['pɔpʌp] *v.* 弹出
[12] **website**：['websait] *n.* 网站
[13] **browse**：[brauz] *v.* 浏览
[14] **etc.**：等等

[15] **brand new**：崭新的
[16] **global**：['gləubəl] *adj.* 全球的
[17] **museum**：[mju(:)'ziəm] *n.* 博物馆

[18] **resources**：resource [ri'zɔ:s] 的复数，*n.* 资源
[19] **FTP server**：文件传输服务器
[20] **download**：['daunləud] *v.* 下载
[21] **marvelous**：['mɑ:viləs] *adj.* 神奇的
[22] **entertainments**：entertainment [,entə'teinmənt] 的复数，*n.* 娱乐

[23] **popular**：['pɔpjulə] *adj.* 流行的
[24] **service provider**：服务供应商

So I press the **power button**, open my computer. After several seconds' waiting, I input my **user name** and **password**. Then, I see a flag which is the **logo** of **Microsoft** and the English words "**Windows XP**". OK! I see "**Internet Explorer**" on the **desktop**! I can go to the Internet now! I **click** the icon of IE, then a **window popup**. I input some **website** address as my teacher taught me, then I can really **browse** some websites. I almost can find everything on Net—news, music, pictures, videos and **etc.**.

The Internet is like a world for me! It's quite different from the world we are living. It's a **brand new** world for me!

For me, the Internet is a **global museum**, a huge mine of knowledge. When I need to look for some data, I will input www.google.com.hk or www.baidu.com in my Internet Explorer, then fill in the keywords. Even without waiting, I can see many searching results concerning the keywords. Maybe there're a lot of **resources** in some **FTP server** for me to **download**.

The Internet is also a **marvelous** palace of **entertainments** for me. I can play some simple flash games myself, also play chess or cards games with unknown people from everywhere, even play a huge game with tens of thousands of people all over the world at the same time. At my hometown, www.gametea.com is a **popular** chess and cards games **service provider**. Almost at any time, many people are playing games on it.

Also, I can express my opinions in the Internet. Many BBS are already open, whether it's all-round or professional, I am always absorbed by some of them. For example, I often visit the BBS of our school, I can talk about anything I want only if it's **legal**. Also I can exchange viewpoints and discuss with many net friends concerning a focused **topic**.

For many young people including me, the Internet is the best place to make friends. Several decades ago, people began to use E-mails to communicate, E-mails can reach any corners in the world in several seconds. In recent years, with the popularity of **broadband network**, instant chatting tools are becoming more and more common, **ICQ、QQ、MSN、WeChat** all become one popular word in our daily life. Take myself as an example, I use QQ to chat with my family and friends quite often. With the development of the IT technology, people can do more and more things on Net, the world has been, is being and will be changed by the Internet in the past, at present and in the future!

[1] **legal**：['li:gəl] *adj*. 合法的

[2] **topic**：['tɔpik] *n*. 主题

[3] **broadband network**：宽带网络

[4] **ICQ**：*abbr*. 世界最流行的即时通信工具软件之一，取意 I seek you

[5] **MSN**：微软公司提供的网络即时通信工具软件

[6] **WeChat**：腾讯公司提供的智能终端即时通信应用程序

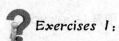

Exercises 1：

Speaking: Make a self-introduction with your own words to your classmates in English (50~80 words).

Writing: Write down your first Net experience with your own words in English (50~80 words).

## Notes

(1) 李丽莎,"陈、周、张、郭、刘、李"等中文姓氏,中国港台地区常根据粤语音译为 "Chan、Chow、Cheung、Kwok、Lau、Lee",如刘德华英文名为 Andy Lau。

(2) E-commerce 是 Electronic Commerce,即"电子商务"的缩写,类似的还有 E-mail 是 Electronic Mail,即"电子邮件"的缩写,有人戏称为"伊妹儿"。

(3) PRC 的全称是 People's Republic of China,即中华人民共和国。

(4) inconvenient 不方便的,不便利的;反义词 convenient 方便的,便利的。"in"是反义前缀,表示与原词相反的意思。

(5) manage 经营、管理,其名词形式是 management,另一名词形式是 manager 经理(表示职务)。

(6) Microsoft 是 micro(微小的)与 soft(软)组成的复合词,中文译为微软,为全球最大的软件(中国港台地区称为"软体")企业,是 Windows 系统的开发商。

(7) FTP server 文件传输服务器,供用户上传和下载文件。

(8) service provider 服务供应商,ISP(Internet Service Provider)表示互联网服务供应商。

(9) BBS 电子布告栏系统(Bulletin Board System),电子公告板,论坛。

(10) ICQ 世界最流行的即时通信工具软件,取意 I seek you。

## Tips for Translation

(1) 当翻译英语中的一些特定词汇时,对于在汉语中已经广泛接受的词汇可以直接用原文表示,比如"IE""Word""Excel"等。

Internet Explorer

(2) 对于一些合成词,则可以直接合成其源词的含义,如"businessman"就可以直接翻译成"商人"。

(3) 对于以"er"或"or"等字母组合结尾的词汇大都是表示做前面那个单词所表示动作的人、机构或设备,如"server"就表示服务器。

(4) 对于以"in"或"im"等字母组合开头的词汇大都是后面那个单词所表示含义的反义词,如"inconvenient"就是"convenient"的反义词。

(5) 将英语语句直接翻译成汉语语句后,要根据中文的习惯调整语序,使其符合中文的表达习惯。如"Also I can exchange viewpoints and discuss with many net friends concerning a focus topic"直接翻译成"也我可以交换看法并讨论和许多网友关于共同关心的话题",这显然不符合中文的表达习惯。因此,将它整理为"我也可以与许多网友就共同关心的话题交换、讨论各自的看法"。

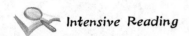 Intensive Reading

## What a Wonderful Net!

[1] **originated**: originate [ə'ridʒineit] 的过去式, v. 起源于
[2] **ARPANET**: 美国国防部高级研究计划署网络
[3] **protocol**: ['prəutəkɔl] n. 协议
[4] **TCP/IP**: 网络的一组通信协议
[5] **marking**: mark [mɑ:k] 的 ing 形式, v. 标志着
[6] **doubled**: double ['dʌbl] 的过去分词形式, v. 双倍, 翻倍

[7] **developed**: develope [di'veləp] 的过去分词形式, v. 开发, 发展
[8] **global**: ['gləubəl] adj. 全世界的
[9] **extremely**: [iks'tri:mli] adv. 非常地
[10] **abundant**: [ə'bʌndənt] adj. 丰富的
[11] **information**: [,infə'meiʃən] n. 信息
[12] **mine**: [main] n. 宝库
[13] **imagine**: [i'mædʒin] v. 想象

[14] **CCTV**: abbr. 中国中央电视台
[15] **consult**: [kən'sʌlt] v. 查阅
[16] **forecast**: ['fɔ:kɑ:st] n. 预测, 预报
[17] **send**: [send] v. 送, 寄, 发送

[18] **CHINANET**: abbr. 中国原邮电部建设的公用主干网
[19] **CERNET**: abbr. 中国教育与科研网

The Internet **originated** from **ARPANET** net in USA, 1960s. On January 1, 1983, the core networking **protocol** of ARPANET was changed to **TCP/IP**, **marking** the start of the Internet as we know it today. From then on, the size of the Internet has **doubled** and doubled by each year. In the beginning, it's only about 200 computers connected to the Internet, and by now it's about tens of millions of computers connected with it, and it has **developed** from USA to the world, and become a really huge **global** network.

The Internet has **extremely abundant** resources of **information**, it's a huge information **mine** for human beings, and it's bigger than you can **imagine**. People can make resources sharing, inter-communication and long-distance teaching and so on in the Internet. For example, you can read the books of the libraries at home; you can go to the **CCTV** website to **consult** the program **forecast** even watch some programs on line; you can **send** mails, photos, music to your friends far away; shop in the Net, learn in the net school, and etc..

In China, the number of the users of the Internet has developed to tens of millions, **CHINANET** and **CERNET** have become the main networks.

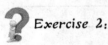 Exercise 2:

List at least 5 famous websites addresses in English.

## Notes

(1) ARPANET   Advanced Research Projects Agency Network，即(美国国防部)高级研究计划署网络。

(2) TCP/IP   用于网络的一组通信协议，包括 IP(Internet Protocol)和 TCP(Transmission Control Protocol)等协议。

(3) CCTV   China Central Television，即中国中央电视台。

(4) CHINANET   中国原邮电部建设的公用主干网，现属于中国电信运营。

(5) CERNET   China Education and Research Network，即中国教育与科研网。

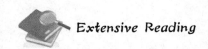

## Extensive Reading

### Shop and Brand

A shop is a place where we can shop, and we call the act "shopping". I like shopping very much, because in the shops I can seek a lot of **commodities** from many different regions in the world. I like Nike shoes **designed** in USA, SONY PSP made in Japan, and LINING baseball cap **manufactured** in China. Among all the brands, I like adidas most, because I **appreciate** the **spirit** of it —"all days I dream about sports!" You see? Adidas is from the first letter of each word in this sentence. How about your **favorite** brand?

A Brand is very important for an **enterprise** in our **society** nowadays. When we go to a market to buy something, we see many different kinds of products of a certain commodity. How can we **differ** them one **from** another? A brand is the easiest way to make it. SONY,

[1] **commodities**: commodity [kə'mɔditi] 的复数, n. 商品

[2] **designed**: design [di'zain] 的过去分词形式, v. 设计

[3] **manufactured**: manufacture [,mænju'fæktʃə] 的过去分词形式, v. 制造

[4] **appreciate**: [ə'pri:ʃieit] v. 欣赏

[5] **spirit**: ['spirit] n. 精神

[6] **favorite**: ['feivərit] adj. 喜爱的

[7] **enterprise**: ['entəpraiz] n. 企业

[8] **society**: [sə'saiəti] n. 社会

[9] **differ from**: 不同于, 与……有区别

Panasonic, TOSHIBA, HITACHI are all brands from Japan, and they all produce TV sets. But many people will consider SONY is the best among them, just because of their **impression** from its brand.

Also, brands make huge **commercial value**. One pair of shoes will be sold at a higher price marked with "Nike" than "LINING". Sometimes, the reason for the price difference is the brand only.

[1] **impression**: [im'preʃən] *n.* 印象

[2] **commercial value**: 商业价值

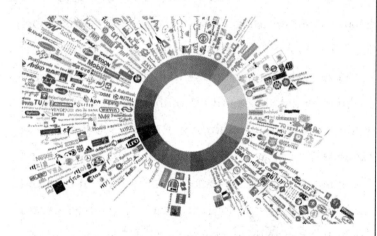

In China, there are still many **OEMs**. They are making products marked with foreign brands and **sharing** a small **portion** of the total **profits**. Hope one day in the future, we Chinese can have many top brands in the world!

[3] **OEMs**: *abbr.* 初始设备制造厂家（Original Equipment Manufacturers 的缩写）

[4] **sharing**: share ['ʃɛər] 的 ing 形式, *v.* 分享

[5] **portion**: ['pɔːʃən] *n.* 部分

[6] **profits**: profit ['prɔfit] 的复数, *n.* 利润

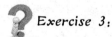 Exercise 3:

List some commodities from famous brands you know.

For example: I know mobile phones from Apple.

 Related Links

## Alipay

**(Sources:** http://ab.alipay.com/i/jieshao.htm#en**)**

Launched in 2004, Alipay (www.alipay.com) is a commonly used third-party online payment solution in China. Alipay provides an **escrow** payment service that reduces **transaction** risk for online consumers. Shoppers have the ability to verify whether they are happy with goods before releasing funds to the seller. On November 11, 2013, Alipay set a record for the highest daily number of transactions, processing 188 million payments during a 24-hour period. 45.18 million of those transactions, with a total transaction **volume** of RMB11.3 billion, were **facilitated** by mobile devices. In June 2013, Alipay and Tianhong Asset Management Co. jointly introduced Yu'e Bao as a way for individuals to manage **excess** funds in their Alipay accounts. Users making **investments** through Yu'e Bao can receive a reasonable level of daily yields and are allowed to **withdraw** their funds anytime.

In November 2013, Alipay's mobile application, Alipay Wallet, started operating as an **independent** brand. In addition to supporting online money transfers, utility payments as well as **offline** purchases at retail stores, cinemas, convenience stores, supermarkets and more, Alipay Wallet also features a built-in Yu'E Bao interface to enable users to manage their investments on the go.

[1] **escrow**：['eskrəu] n. 第三方支付
[2] **transaction**：[træn'zækʃ(ə)n] n. 交易
[3] **volume**：['vɔljuːm] n. 量
[4] **facilitated**：facilitate [fə'siliteit] 的过去分词形式，v. 促进，帮助，使容易
[5] **excess**：[ik'ses] adj. 额外的，过量的，附加的
[6] **investments**：investment [in'vestmənt] 的复数，n. [经] 投资，投资的财产
[7] **withdraw**：[wið'drɔː] v. 撤退，撤销，取款
[8] **independent**：[,indi'pendənt] adj. 独立的，单独的
[9] **offline**：[ɔf'lain] adj. 线下的，脱机的，离线的

Alipay partners with multiple **financial institutions** including leading national and regional banks across China as well as Visa and MasterCard to facilitate payments in China and abroad. Apart from Taobao Marketplace and Tmall.com, Alipay provides payment **solutions** to merchants in **a wide range of** industries including online retail, virtual gaming, digital communications, commercial services, air ticketing and utilities. It also offers an online payment solution to help merchants worldwide sell directly to consumers in China and supports transactions in 14 major foreign **currencies**.

[1] **financial institutions**：金融机构

[2] **solutions**：solution [sə'luʃən] 的复数，n. 解决方案

[3] **a wide range of**：大范围的，许多各种不同的

[4] **currencies**：currency ['kʌr(ə)nsi] 的复数，n. 货币，通货

### Exercise 4:

Choose the best option and fill in the bracket with the mark No..

1. The biggest network in the world is (   ).

   A. Intranet                B. Internet
   C. WWW                     D. Chinanet

2. Which of the following file type is NOT a web page file? (   )

   A. html                    B. htm
   C. shtml                   D. zip

3. The most important input device that we used to surf www is (   ).

   A. keyboard                B. mouse
   C. scanner                 D. printer

4. The protocol of ADSL is (   ).

   A. PPPOE                   B. PPP
   C. TCP                     D. IP

5. The protocol system of Internet is (   ).

   A. IPX                     B. TCP/IP
   C. SPX                     D. TCP/UDP

6. The most frequent file type of www picture is (   ).

   A. bmp                     B. tif
   C. jpg                     D. pdf

7. Which of the following softwares is NOT a web browser? (   )

   A. IE                      B. Firefox
   C. Chrome                  D. Flashget

8. The most famous C2C website in China is (   ).

   A. taobao.com              B. ebay.com
   C. youa.baidu.com          D. paipai.com

9. The most valuable IT company in the world is (   ).

   A. Facebook                B. Google
   C. Apple                   D. Samsung

10. The biggest PC provider in the world is (   ).

    A. Lenovo                 B. Dell
    C. Acer                   D. HP

参考译文及答案

# 单元一　神奇网络

博客

## 我能在互联网上做什么

大家好！我叫李丽莎，今年19岁，是中华人民共和国浙江省温州市一所不错的职业学院的大二学生，我的专业是电子商务。

今天是星期六，外面下起了大雨。因为今天没上课，原本我可以出去在城市里逛一圈。如果可能，我还想买本叫做《大数据时代：生活、工作与思想的大变革》的书。但是我讨厌雨天外出，因为我骑车不方便，坐公交车也不方便。当然打的会好些，可是那太贵了，我可没钱哦。

我的父母工作很辛苦，他们几乎从来没有节假日。他们都是商人，每天忙着经营他们的商店，连周末也不例外。他们甚至认为周末是他们生意的高峰期。因此，他们周末没有时间和我在一起。由于下大雨，一个愉快的假日眼看着就要变成无聊的一天了！

我开始想怎么在学习5天后度过我的假日。复习功课？不，至少不是今天早上！外面的雨下得更大了，我不出去又能做什么呢？哦，对了！为什么不上网冲浪呢？

于是我按下了电源按钮，打开我的电脑。几秒钟的等待过后，我输入了我的用户名和密码。然后，我看见一幅带有微软图标的旗帜和"Windows XP"英语单词的画面。好！我看见桌面上有"IE"！我现在可以上网了！我单击了IE的图标，一个窗口弹出。我输入了一些老师教给我们的网址，然后我就可以真正浏览网页了。我几乎可以在网络上找到一切——新闻、音乐、图片等。

互联网对我而言就像是一个世界！一个与我们生活的世界相当不同的世界。这对我来讲是一个崭新的世界！

对我而言，互联网是一个全球博物馆，一个知识的宝藏。当我需要查找资料时，我就在我的IE里输入www.google.com.hk或www.baidu.com，然后再输入关键词。甚至不需要等待，我就可以看到许多关于这些关键词的搜索结果。可能在FTP服务器上还有大量的资源可供我下载。

互联网对我也是一个娱乐的奇妙宫殿。我可以玩一些简单的在线小游戏，也可以和一些网络上不认识的人玩一些棋牌游戏，甚至可以同时和全世界各地的上万人来玩一个大型的游戏。在我的家乡，游戏茶苑是一个很受欢迎的棋牌游戏服务供应商。几乎在任何时间，都有许多人在上面玩游戏。

同时，我可以在互联网上表达我自己的观点。许多众论或专业的BBS均已开放，我经常会被其中的某些东西吸引。比如，我经常访问我们学校的BBS，我可以谈论任何合法的话题。我也可以与许多网友讨论共同关心的话题，交换各自的看法。

对许多包括我在内的年轻人来讲，互联网是交朋友的好地方。几十年以前，人们开始使用电子邮件互相沟通，电子邮件可以在数秒内到达世界的任何角落。近些年来，随着宽带网络的普及，即时聊天工具变得越来越寻常，ICQ、QQ、MSN 和微信都变成了我们日常生活中的流行词汇。以我自己为例，我经常用 QQ 与家人和朋友聊天。随着信息技术的发展，人们可在网络上做越来越多的事情，世界过去已经、现在正在并且将在未来被互联网所改变！

精读

### 多么奇妙的网络啊

互联网起源于 20 世纪 60 年代美国的 ARPANET。在 1983 年 1 月 1 日，ARPANET 的核心协议转变为 TCP/IP，成为我们今日所知的互联网的开端。从那时起，互联网的规模每年翻番。起初，只有大约 200 台电脑与互联网相连，到如今已经有几千万台电脑联网，已经从美国发展到全世界，成为真正巨大的全球网络。

互联网已经成为一个极其丰富的信息资源，成为人类的巨大信息库，比你所能想象的都要大。人们可以在互联网上实现信息分享、互相沟通、远程教学等。比如，你可以在家里实现对图书馆图书的阅读，你可以上中央电视台的网站查询节目预告，甚至可以在线观看节目；你还可以给远方的朋友发送电子邮件、图片和音乐，还可以在线购物、在线学习等。

在中国，互联网用户的数量已经发展到数千万，CHINANET 和 CERNET 已经成为主干网络。

泛读

### 商店与品牌

商店是一个可以购物的地方，我们把这种行为叫做"购物"。我非常喜欢购物。因为我可以在商店里找到许多来自世界不同地区的商品。我喜欢美国设计的耐克鞋，日本制造的索尼游戏机和中国制造的李宁牌棒球帽。在所有的品牌里，我最喜欢阿迪达斯，因为我欣赏它的精神——"我每天都梦想运动！"你知道吗？阿迪达斯由这个句子中每个单词的首字母组合而来。你最喜欢哪个品牌呢？

如今在社会上，品牌对于企业是非常重要的。当我们去市场上买东西时，我们看到了同一种商品的许多不同种类的产品。我们如何把它们同其他的区别开来呢？品牌就是区别的最简单方法。索尼、松下、东芝、日立都是日本的品牌，它们都生产电视机。但许多人会认为索尼是其中最好的，原因仅仅是他们对这个品牌的印象。

此外，品牌可以创造巨大的商业价值。一双"耐克"牌的鞋子就可以比"李宁"牌的鞋子卖得贵。有时候，价格差异的唯一原因就是品牌。

在中国，依然有许多的原始设备制造商（代工）。他们生产的产品标着外国的品牌，只分享到全部利润中的一小部分。希望未来有一天，我们中国人可以拥有许多世界顶尖品牌！

相关链接

### 支付宝

（来源：http://ab.alipay.com/i/jieshao.htm#en）

支付宝（中国）网络技术有限公司是国内领先的第三方支付平台，致力于提供"简单、安全、快速"的支付解决方案。支付宝公司从 2004 年建立开始，始终以"信任"作为产品和服务的核心。作为中国主流的第三方支付平台，它不仅从产品上确保用户在线支付的安全，同时致力于通过担保交易等创新让用户通过支付宝在网络间建立信任的关系，去帮助建设更纯净的互联网环境。截至 2013 年 11 月，支付宝单日交易笔数峰值达到 1.88 亿，其中，移动支付单日交易笔数峰值达到 4518 万，移动支付单日交易额峰值达到 113 亿人民币。2013 年 6 月，支付宝推出账户余额增值服务"余额宝"，通过余额宝，用户不仅能够得到较高的收益，还能随时消费支付和转出，无任何手续费。"一元起售，草根理财"的观念也随之深入人心。

  2013 年 11 月起，支付宝手机客户端"支付宝钱包"宣布成为独立品牌进行运作，将为用户提供更加便捷的移动支付服务。在线下，支付宝钱包不仅内置了余额宝，真正实现了随时随地"移动理财"，更以成熟的账户支付体系和创新的支付解决方案为线下商户提供更加便捷完善的移动支付服务。目前，支付宝钱包"当面付"功能已覆盖零售百货、电影院线、连锁商超、出租车等多个行业。

  从 2004 年建立至今，支付宝及支付宝钱包已经成为线上及线下众多商家首选的支付解决方案，为连接亿万用户及商户提供了基础的资金流服务。支付宝稳健的作风、先进的技术、敏锐的市场预见能力及极大的社会责任感，赢得了银行等合作伙伴的广泛认同。目前，支付宝已经跟国内外 180 多家银行以及 Visa、MasterCard 国际组织等机构建立了深入的战略合作关系，成为金融机构在电子支付领域最为信任的合作伙伴。支付宝会跟各领域的合作伙伴一起，继续围绕用户需求不断创新。希望用支付宝的服务给您的生活带来微小而美好的改变。

练习一　（略）
练习二　（略）
练习三　（略）
练习四　1. B　2. D　3. B　4. A　5. B　6. C　7. D　8. A　9. C　10. A

# Unit Two
## Online Shopping

Blog: Shopping without Going Out!

Intensive Reading: The Development of E-commerce

Extensive Reading: Online Payment

Related Links: McDonald's Goes Online to Sell Consumer Goods

China Eastern Airlines and Alibaba Group Form Strategic Alliance in E-commerce

## *Shopping without Going Out!*

After **visiting** so many websites, one idea comes to my mind. Why not go to a bookstore on Net to buy a book called "Big Data: A Revolution That Will Transform How We Live, Work and Think"? Many classmates of mine have succeeded in buying many **commodities** on Net, such as mobile phones, jeans, watches and sportswear. Oh, yeah, let me have a try myself!

I get on the website of "**Google**", and input "bookstore" as my key words for search. 0.19 seconds later, thousands and thousands of bookstores' website addresses show on my **monitor**. Among them, I choose www.amazon.com because the name **rings a bell**. Amazon is an American electronic commerce company based in **Seattle**. It was one of the first major companies to sell goods on the Internet. Amazon also owns Alexa Internet, a9.com, and the Internet Movie Database (IMDb). I have heard it's the biggest Net bookstore in the world. On the **homepage** of Amazon, I find so many books' **brief introduction**. In order to search the book, I input "Big Data" for searching, soon I get it! In fact, Amazon is a huge bookstore without shops! It's so funny!

Amazon Net bookstore was **founded** in 1995, which is an example of global E-commerce success. Visitors can shop millions of sorts of English books, audios, videos on it.

Since 1999, Amazon began to **enlarge** the sorts of the commodities they sold. Besides books and audios & videos, they also sell electronics, **apparel**, **gifts**, **toys**,

[1] **visiting**: ['vizitiŋ] *v*. 访问

[2] **commodities**: commodity [kə'mɔditi] 的复数，*n*. 商品，货物

[3] **Google**: *n*. 谷歌，全球最著名的搜索网站

[4] **monitor**: ['mɔnitə] *n*. 监视器，电脑显示器

[5] **rings a bell**: 声名远扬，如雷贯耳

[6] **Seattle**: [si'ætl] *n*. 西雅图

[7] **homepage**: ['həumpeidʒ] *n*. 主页，首页

[8] **brief introduction**: 简要介绍

[9] **founded**: found [faund] 的过去分词形式，*v*. 建立

[10] **enlarge**: [in'lɑːdʒ] *v*. 扩大，增大
[11] **apparel**: [ə'pærəl] *n*. 衣服，装具
[12] **gifts**: gift [gift] 的复数，*n*. 礼物
[13] **toys**: toy [tɔi] 的复数，*n*. 玩具

[1] **home electrical appliances**：家用电器
[2] **categories**：category [ˈkætigəri] 的复数，n. 类别
[3] **quarter**：[ˈkwɔːtə] n. 季度
[4] **sales**：sale [seil] 的复数，n. 销售额
[5] **billion**：[ˈbiljən] n. 十亿
[6] **reliable**：[riˈlaiəbl] adj. 可靠的，可信的
[7] **payment**：[ˈpeimənt] n. 支付
[8] **Mainland**：[ˈmeinlənd] n. 大陆
[9] **www.baidu.com**：n. 百度网
[10] **www.dangdang.com**：n. 当当网
[11] **comprehendsive**：[ˌkɔmpriˈhensiv] adj. 综合的
[12] **Mall**：[mɔːl] n. 商场
[13] **investing institutions**：投资机构
[14] **American Tiger Fund**：美国老虎基金
[15] **American IDG Group**：美国国际数据集团
[16] **operation**：[ˌɔpəˈreiʃən] n. 运转，经营
[17] **maintained**：maintain [meinˈtein] 的过去分词形式，v. 保持，维持
[18] **cosmetics**：cosmetic [kɔzˈmetik] 的复数，n. 化妆品
[19] **digitals**：digital [ˈdidʒitəl] 的复数，n. 数码产品
[20] **exceeded**：exceed [ikˈsiːd] 的过去分词形式，v. 超过，超越
[21] **surpassed**：surpass [səˈpɑːs] 的过去分词形式，v. 超过，多于
[22] **registers**：register [ˈredʒistə] 的复数，n. 注册者

**home electrical appliances** and etc., totally about 20 **categories**.

For the last **quarter** of 2013, the net **sales** of Amazon reached US$25.59 **billion**, increased 20% over the same period of the previous year. The net profit is US$239 million for this period, and the data for the same period of last year is US$97 million, which increased 146%. The net sales of Amazon in 2013 reached US$74.45 billion, which made a growth of 22% over US$61.09 billion in 2012.

After reading some background about Amazon, I think it should be a **reliable** website for shopping. I find the book "Big Data: A Revolution That Will Transform How We Live, Work and Think" in Amazon soon, but I meet a problem when I want to pay, Amazon doesn't accept the **payment** from **Mainland** China! Unfortunately, I have to search a new E-commerce website on **www.baidu.com**, I get **www.dangdang.com.**

The www.dangdang.com was once the biggest **comprehendsive** Chinese Net Shopping **Mall**, invested by some famous **investing institutions** such as **American Tiger Fund** and **American IDG Group** and etc.. Its **operation** started in Nov. 1999. Since the founding, it has **maintained** a growing rate of 100% each year, and reached 120% in 2009. The commodities sold on line by dangdang include books, videos, **cosmetics, digitals** and etc., the sorts has **exceeded** 1,000,000, the kinds of books in stock has **surpassed** 600,000. The number of new **registers** is still increasing each year, they are from all over China. More than 10,000 people shop everyday, more than 30 million people browse all kinds of information every month on www.dangdang.com, more than 20 million pieces of commodities are sold through the website monthly.

It's a very big Net bookstore of China, the sales has even surpassed the most famous bookstore "**xinhua bookstore**". Also I can buy the same book here. At the same time, I see many **comments** on this book. Someone say it is a must-read for anyone who wants to **stay ahead of** one of the key trends defining the future of business. Someone say it **breaks new ground** in identifying how today's **avalanche** of information fundamentally shifts our basic understanding of the world. Argued boldly and written beautifully, the book clearly shows how companies can unlock value, how **policymakers** need to be on guard, and how everyone's **cognitive** models need to change. How can I pay to buy the book?

[1] **xinhua bookstore**：新华书店

[2] **comments**：comment ['kɔment] 的复数，*n*. 评论，意见

[3] **stay ahead of**：走在……的前面，比……领先

[4] **breaks new ground**：开辟新天地

[5] **avalanche**：['ævəlɑːnʃ] *n*. 雪崩，似雪崩的事物

[6] **policymakers**：决策者

[7] **cognitive**：['kɔgnitiv] *adj*. 认知的，认识的

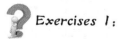 Exercises 1：

Speaking: Express your feelings about your first Net shopping experience in English (50~80 words).

Writing: Write down your first Net shopping procedure with your own words in English (50~80 words).

## Notes

(1) homepage 主页，通过万维网进行信息查询的起始信息页。

(2) home electrical appliances 家用电器。

(3) categories 类别。

(4) quarter 四分之一，一刻钟，季度。

(5) net sales 净销售额，是指销售额减去退货后的净值。

(6) billion 十亿。英语中没有"万"，只有"千"(thousand)、"百万"(million)。

(7) Big Data: A Revolution That Will Transform How We Live, Work and Think 《大数据时代：生活、工作与思想的大变革》，是目前全球最热销的书之一。

(8) American IDG Group 美国国际数据集团，是著名的高科技投资企业，投资于中国众多的知名网络企业。

## Tips for Translation

(1) 当翻译英语中的某些以"es"结尾的词汇时，可以根据语法规则去推测它的原型再来翻译，比如"commodities"是"commodity"的复数形式，是将"y"改成"i"再加"es"的结果，其含义是"商品"。

(2) "electron"是"电子"的意思，"electronic"表示"电子的"，"electronics"表示"电子学、电子设备"；"electricity"是"电、电气"的意思，"electric"表示"电的、电气的"，"electrical"表示"用电的"，"electrical equipment/appliance"表示"电器"。

(3) "quarter"本义是"四分之一"，所以它可以表示"一刻钟"（一小时的四分之一），也可以表示"一季度"（一年的四分之一）。

(4) increase、surpass(exceed)常见于商务英语中，含义分别是增长、超越，一般用于描述市场份额、营业额、利润等商业指标的前后对比。

(5) 某些来自汉语拼音的英语词汇，可以直接用其汉语原文去翻译；但是将汉语翻译成英语时，地名、人名等专有名词只可音译不可意译，比如温州市最著名的商业街"五马街"只可翻译成"Wuma Street"，不可翻译成"Five Horses Street"。

## Intensive Reading

### The Development of E-commerce

[1] **mail order**：邮购
[2] **TV shopping**：电视购物
[3] **telephone shopping**：电话购物

In the past, people liked to shop in shops, markets, supermarkets and malls. When we did it, we must go to some places ourselves. Later, people make some new shopping ways such as **mail order**, **TV shopping** and **telephone shopping** and so on. The commodities we bought will be sent to the addresses we **specify**.

[4] **specify**：['spesifai] v. 指定

[5] **unbelievable**：[ˌʌnbi'li:vəbl] adj. 难以置信的

[6] **Dell**：戴尔
[7] **consumers**：consumer [kən'sju:mə] 的复数，n. 顾客

In recent years, the Internet has developed at an **unbelievable** speed, and people also began to think how to sell goods on the Net without shops. For example, some famous companies like Amazon, **Dell**, they began to sell their products to **consumers** on the Internet when they were still nothing not long ago. They've won a great success in E-commerce! This type is called **B2C**, similar to Net **retailing**.

[8] **B2C**：abbr. Business to Consumer 的简写，企业对消费者的电子商务模式
[9] **retailing**：['ri:teiliŋ] n. 零售业

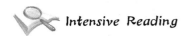

[10] **increasingly**：[in'kri:siŋli] adv. 日益，越来越多地，不断增加地
[11] **well-educated**：['wel'edju:keitid] adj. 受过良好教育的
[12] **youths**：youth [ju:θ] 的变形，n. 年轻人
[13] **SARS**：abbr. 非典型肺炎（简称非典）
[14] **Canton Fair**：广交会（中国进出口商品交易会）

The business done through the Internet is called "E-commerce" and it's **increasingly** accepted by more and more people, especially **well-educated youths**. When **SARS** happened in China, many foreign buyers planning to visit the **Canton Fair** changed their ideas and **purchased** from Chinese **suppliers** online instead of coming themselves. At that time, Alibaba got a big progress and accepted by more and more **enterprises**. Alibaba offers a **platform** for both sellers and buyers to search and **transact** the goods they are interested. This type is called **B2B**, similar to Net **wholesaling**. Also, Taobao offers a platform for an **individual** to buy and sell, the type is called **C2C**, similar to Net retailing between consumers.

[1] **purchased**: purchase ['pɜːtʃəs] 的过去式，v. 购买，采购
[2] **suppliers**: supplier [sə'plaɪə] 的复数，n. 供应者，供货商
[3] **enterprises**: enterprise ['entəpraɪz] 的复数，n. 企业
[4] **platform**: ['plætfɔːm] n. 平台
[5] **transact**: [træn'zækt] v. 交易，谈判
[6] **B2B**: abbr. Business to Business 的简写，企业对企业的电子商务模式
[7] **wholesaling**: ['həʊseɪlɪŋ] n. 批发
[8] **individual**: [ˌɪndɪ'vɪdjʊəl] n. 个人
[9] **C2C**: abbr. Consumer to Consumer 的简写，消费者对消费者的电子商务模式

With the **popularity** of the Internet, we believe that E-Commerce will develop faster than ever.

[10] **popularity**: [ˌpɒpjə'lærɪti] n. 普遍，流行

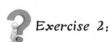 Exercise 2:

List at least 5 famous E-commerce websites in English.

## Notes

(1) unbelievable 难以置信的。"un+believe+able",由 believe 加 able 构成形容词,再加 un 变成反义词。

(2) Dell 戴尔(戴尔电脑公司及其创始人的姓氏)。

(3) B2C Business to Consumer 企业到用户的电子商务模式(也称商家对个人客户或商业机构对消费者,也就是电子商务商业机构对消费者的电子商务,基本等同于企业电子商务零售)。

(4) SARS Severe Acute Respiratory Syndrome 严重急性呼吸道综合征,俗称非典型肺炎,简称非典。

(5) Canton Fair 广交会,也称为 Guangzhou Fair,全称为 "China Import and Export Fair",中国进出口商品交易会,是我国规模最大的国际经贸盛会。

(6) B2B Business to Business,企业对企业的电子商务模式,基本等同于企业电子商务批发。

(7) individual 个别的,单独的,个人的;独特的;一个人的,供一人用的;与众不同的;独特的,特殊的,个性的,有特性的;个人的,个体的;*n.*,个人;[口语]人(常指有趣或有点特别的人);与众不同的人,有个性的人;某种类型的人,(尤指)古怪的人。

(8) C2C 即 Consumer To Consumer,消费者对消费者的电子商务模式,基本等同于个人电子商务零售。

 **Extensive Reading**

## Online Payment

Different from the **traditional** shopping, buyers can't pay the sellers face to face. So Net shopping depends on online banks to **accomplish** payments and the third-party online payment platforms to **guarantee security**.

The online bank is to connect the customers' **terminal** with the banks' through the Internet, to **realize** the banking service reach to the customers' office or home, make the customers not limited by the business hours, manage their **accounts** in the bank without outgoing.

By now, many commercial banks have already opened their Net banking service. It's very **convenient** for people to shop on Net, they can check their accounts, make a **transfer**, pay a **loan** and etc. at home. But before you use the service, you must **apply for** opening the service. Usually, on the homepages of many banks, they offer the links to their net banking service.

[1] **traditional**：[trə'diʃənəl] adj. 传统的
[2] **accomplish**：[ə'kɔmpliʃ] v. 完成
[3] **guarantee**：[ˌɡærən'tiː] v. 保证
[4] **security**：[si'kjuːriti] n. 安全

[5] **terminal**：['təːminl] n. 终端
[6] **realize**：['riəlaiz] v. 实现

[7] **accounts**：account [ə'kaunt] 的复数，n. 账号

[8] **convenient**：[kən'viːnjənt] adj. 方便的

[9] **transfer**：[træns'fəː] n. 转移，转账
[10] **loan**：[ləun] n. 贷款
[11] **apply for**：申请

[1] **keep alert**：保持警惕
[2] **measures**：measure ['meʒəz] 的复数，*n.* 措施
[3] **virus**：['vaiərəs] *n.* 病毒
[4] **Trojan backdoor**：*n.* 特洛伊木马病毒
[5] **loss**：[lɔs] *n.* 损失
[6] **appear**：[ə'piə] *v.* 出现
[7] **Alipay**：支付宝
[8] **escrow**：['eskrəu] *n.* 第三方，契约
[9] **offered**：offer ['ɔfə] 的过去分词形式，*v.* 提供
[10] **procedure**：[prə'si:dʒə] *n.* 步骤

For the safety of using the Net banking service, we have to **keep alert** always besides the security **measures** offered by the banks. If you get the computer **virus** containing **Trojan backdoor**, your bank account and your password is probably stolen, by then the **loss** will possibly **appear**.

**Alipay** is an **escrow** service **offered** by Alibaba Group that helps protect payments when buying and selling on Alibaba.com and Taobao.com. The **procedure** is: buyer orders online, buyer payment secured, supplier ships order, buyer confirms delivery, supplier receives payment. Now Alipay is most popular online payment system in China, has solved the credit problem between sellers and buyers successfully.

 **Exercise 3：**

List at least 5 bank names in English.

For example: Bank of China.

 Related Links

## McDonald's Goes Online to Sell Consumer Goods

(Sources: April 28, 2009, By WSJ Staff, From China Journal's Juliet Yet)

In February, McDonald's launched an online shop on Alibaba's Taobao, China's top online **auction** site, to promote its Super Value meal. The fast-food giant wasn't selling **burgers**. Instead, for two months it sold popular and fashionable products such as mobile phones, digital cameras and MP3 players on its **virtual** store, along with the more **predictable** gift **vouchers**. Many gifts were sold at **promotional**, **discounted** prices.

The McDonald's Super Value online store was the chain's first online shop, according to Phyllis Cheung, chief marketing officer of McDonald's China. "It's a **strategic** media tactic to **target** the right **audience**," she said— specifically, urban **adults** in their 20s.

Other major brands, such as Procter & Gamble, Dell, Lenovo and Samsung have set up e-stores on Taobao. Skyworth, a major Chinese TV producer, and Digital China Holdings, a large IT products **distributor** in China, **partnered** with Baidu Youa for their online

[1] **auction**：[ˈɔːkʃən] n. 拍卖

[2] **burgers**：burger [bəːgə] 的复数，n. 汉堡

[3] **virtual**：[ˈvəːtjuəl] adj. 虚拟的

[4] **predictable**：[priˈdiktəbl] adj. 可预知的

[5] **vouchers**：voucher [ˈvautʃə] 的复数，n. 代金券

[6] **promotional**：[prəuˈməuʃənəl] adj. 促销

[7] **discounted**：[ˈdiskauntid] adj. 有折扣的

[8] **strategic**：[strəˈtiːdʒik] adj. 战略的

[9] **target**：[ˈtɑːgit] v. 把……作为目标

[10] **audience**：[ˈɔːdjəns] n. 受众，拥护者

[11] **adults**：adult [ˈædʌlt] 的复数，n. 成年人

[12] **distributor**：[disˈtribjutə] n. 经销商

[13] **partnered**：partner [ˈpɑːtnə] 的过去式，v. 合作，搭档

businesses. One recent entrant is **Uniqlo** Co., a casual wear brand under Japan's leading apparel retail group Fast Retailing Co., Ltd. Last week, Uniqlo announced a partnership with Taobao to launch set up a virtual **flagship store**.

McDonald's used an auction system to promote its Value Meals. It **posted** electronic goods on its Taobao site for close to the **retail price**, but **dropped** the price when a user clicked on it. The first user to click on it at the price of 16.5 yuan — the price of a Value Meal, or **roughly** $2.50 — got to buy the item at that price.

McDonald's has targeted China as a major growth area. At present, McDonald's **operates** over 1,000 restaurants in China and plans to open roughly 150 new restaurants this year. Earlier this year, it also cut the prices on about 40% of its items by as much as a third.

[1] **Uniqlo**：优衣库（日本服饰品牌）
[2] **flagship store**：旗舰店
[3] **posted**：post [pəust] 的过去式，v. 发布
[4] **retail price**：零售价
[5] **dropped**：drop [drɔp] 的过去式，v. 降低
[6] **roughly**：['rʌfli] adv. 概略地
[7] **operates**：operate ['ɔpəreit] 的第三人称单数，v. 经营

## *China Eastern Airlines and Alibaba Group Form Strategic Alliance in E-commerce*

(Sources: http://www.abnnewswire.net)

Shanghai, Nov. 24, 2009 (ABN Newswire)—China Eastern Airlines, a **leading carrier** in China, has formed a **strategic alliance** with Alibaba Group's Alipay and Taobao **subsidiaries** to expand China Eastern's capability to serve more customers through E-commerce. Under the alliance, Alipay will provide online payment support for ticket sales on the China Eastern website (www.ceair.com). China Eastern will also launch

[1] **leading**：['li:diŋ] adj. 领导的
[2] **carrier**：['kæriə] n. 承运商
[3] **strategic alliance**：战略联盟
[4] **subsidiaries**：subsidiary [səb'sidiəri] 的复数，n. 子公司

a flagship store on Taobao Mall to sell tickets **directly** to customers for all **domestic flight routes**.

"Direct online ticket sales is **economical** and convenient, thereby making it the most ideal way for a modern airline carrier to give back to its customers," said Ma Xulun, general manager of China Eastern Airlines. "Through E-commerce, China Eastern **aims** to improve its **ratio** of direct ticket sales and thereby its **competitive advantage** in the marketplace. **Additional** online sales channels and online payment methods will help the airline save on **operational** costs as well as improve the **efficiency** of **capital investments**."

"Alipay is proud to provide secure third-party online payment support to the China Eastern website while also supporting its flagship online store on Taobao Mall," added Shao Xiaofeng, **president** of Alipay. "It is a **priority** for Alipay to continue to set the industry standard in providing safety and security

[1] **directly**：[di'rektli] *adv.* 直接地
[2] **domestic**：[də'mestik] *adj.* 国内的
[3] **flight routes**：航线
[4] **economical**：[ˌiːkə'nɔmikəl] *adj.* 节俭的，经济的

[5] **aims**：aim [eim] 的第三人称单数，*v.* 旨在
[6] **ratio**：['reiʃiəu] *n.* 比率
[7] **competitive advantage**：竞争优势
[8] **Additional**：[ə'diʃənl] *adj.* 附加的
[9] **operational**：[ˌɔpə'reiʃənl] *adj.* 运作的
[10] **efficiency**：[i'fiʃənsi] *n.* 效率
[11] **capital**：['kæpitl] *n.* 资本
[12] **investments**：investment [in'vestmənt] 的复数，*n.* 投资

[13] **president**：['prezidənt] *n.* 总裁
[14] **priority**：[prai'ɔriti] *n.* 优先

in online payment **transactions** as increasing numbers of companies around the world look to **reach** customers in China through E-commerce."

"As more and more Chinese consumers turn to Taobao to meet all of their lifestyle needs, it is important for Taobao Mall to continually **enhance** its range of quality product offerings," said Jonathan Lu, president of Taobao. "Through the China Eastern store on Taobao Mall, Chinese consumers, including more than 145 million registered Taobao users, will have **access** to the most competitively priced **airfares** and **benefit** from a centralized customer service **portal** that can address their needs at every stage of the shopping experience."

This alliance **highlights** the **macro trend** of **multinational companies** turning to E-commerce to provide greater convenience to existing customers as well expand its customer base. China Eastern Airlines is the latest of the many major companies turning to Taobao Mall and Alipay to grow their businesses and better serve customers across China. Taobao Mall, launched in April 2008, was established as a B2C platform for **corporate retailers** to offer Taobao users greater shopping selection. China Eastern joins the ranks of major international and domestic brands such as Uniqlo, **Procter and Gamble, Bestseller and Lenovo**, who have all launched flagship online retail **storefronts** in Taobao Mall and rely on Alipay to **facilitate** their online payment.

---

[1] **transactions**: transaction [træn'zækʃən] 的复数, *n.* 交易
[2] **reach**: [riːtʃ] *v.* 到达，延伸
[3] **enhance**: [in'hɑːns] *v.* 提高
[4] **access**: ['ækses] *n.* 使用之权，获得
[5] **airfares**: airfare ['ɛəfɛə] 的复数, *n.* 机票价格
[6] **benefit**: ['benifit] *n.* 利益
[7] **portal**: ['pɔːtəl] *n.* 入口，[计]门户
[8] **highlights**: highlight ['hailait] 的第三人称单数, *v.* 使显著，使突出
[9] **macro**: ['mækrəu] *adj.* 巨大的，大范围的
[10] **trend**: [trend] *n.* 趋势
[11] **multinational companies**: 跨国公司
[12] **corporate retailers**: 企业零售商
[13] **Procter and Gamble, Bestseller and Lenovo**: 宝洁，绫致，联想
[14] **storefronts**: *n.* 店面
[15] **facilitate**: [fə'siliteit] *v.* 帮助

## Exercise 4:

Choose the best option and fill in the bracket with the mark No..

1. Rose said that he had never had to contend with any girl as fat as (     ).
A. her            B. hers
C. she            D. herself

2. Many scientists believe that oil was formed in the earth (     ) years ago.
A. million            B. millions
C. million of         D. millions of

3. The officer (     ) his orders to the men by radio.
A. reported           B. transmitted
C. communicated       D. exchanged

4. He's never again written (     ) as his first one.
A. a such good book   B. a so good book
C. so good a book     D. such good a book

5. It wasn't long (     ) he found a job.
A. until              B. before
C. since              D. after

6. There are (     ) benefits in the new system.
A. concise            B. tangible
C. precise            D. metal

7. Was it during the Second World War (     ) he died?
A. that               B. while
C. in which           D. then

8. I (     ) to come over to see you, but someone called and I couldn't get away.
A. intended           B. would intend
C. had intended       D. has intended

9. He (     ) to be a liar but a fool.
A. thinks             B. thinking
C. thought            D. was thought

10. He said he wouldn't mind (     ) at home.
A. leaving alone      B. being left alone
C. to be left lonely  D. to leave alone

## 参考译文及答案

# 单元二　网上购物

博客

### 足不出户去购物

访问了许多网站之后,我的脑海里冒出一个想法——为什么不去网上书店买本《大数据时代:生活、工作与思想的大变革》呢?我的许多同学都成功地在网上买到了许多商品,比如手机、牛仔裤、手表和运动服。哦,我试试看吧!

我上了谷歌,输入关键字"书店",0.19秒后,数以万计的书店网站地址出现在我的显示器上。我在其中选择了亚马逊网站,因为这个名字如雷贯耳。亚马逊是一家位于美国西雅图的电子商务公司,是最早在互联网上卖东西的几大公司之一。亚马逊还拥有Alexa Internet 和 a9.com 以及互联网电影数据库(IMDb)。我曾听说它是世界上最大的网络书店,在它的主页上,我找到了许多图书的简介。为了找到这本书,我输入"Big Data"进行搜索,然后很快就找到了!事实上,亚马逊是一家没有店铺的巨大书店!这真是太有趣了!

亚马逊书店于1995年创立,它是全球电子商务成功的典范。访问者可以在上面购买数百万种英语图书、音频和视频。

自1999年以来,亚马逊开始扩大销售商品的范围。除了图书、音频及视频以外,他们也销售电子产品、服装、礼品、玩具、家用电器等,总计20多个大类。

亚马逊2013年第4季度净销售额为255.9亿美元,同比增长20%;净利润为2.39亿美元,去年同期为9700万美元,同比增长146%;亚马逊2013全年净销售额年增长22%,达744.5亿美元,2012年为610.9亿美元。

在看过这些亚马逊的背景介绍以后,我觉得这是一家可靠的购物网站。我很快就在亚马逊上找到了《大数据时代:生活、工作与思想的大变革》这本书,但是我在支付的时候遇到了一个问题,亚马逊不接受来自中国大陆的付款!没办法,我只好在百度上再搜索一个电子商务网站,我找到了当当网。

当当网曾是最大的中文网上综合购物商城,由一些著名的投资机构投资,包括美国老虎基金和美国国际数据集团等。它于1999年11月开始运营,自建立以来每年都保持了100%的增长率,在2009年达到了120%。当当网出售的商品包括书籍、视频、化妆品、数码产品等,种类已经逾百万,在库图书达到60万种。注册用户数量每年都在增加,他们来自全国各地。每天有上万人在当当网买东西,每月有3000万人在当当网浏览各类信息,当当网每月销售商品超过2000万件。这是中国一个巨大的网上书店,它的销售额已经超过了最著名的书店——"新华书店"。我也可以在这里买到相同的书。与此同时，我看到了许多对该书的评论。有人说，对于那些想在未来商业的关键领域中保持领先地位的人来说，大数据是一本必读的书。也有人说，在厘清现今的爆炸式信息如何从根本上转变我们对世界的基本理解方面，大数据开辟了新天地。它推论大胆、文笔漂亮，清晰地展示了公司如何能够释放潜在的价值，决策者需要如何警惕，以及每个人的认知模型需要如何改变。那么，我怎样才能付款买到这本书呢？

精读

## 电子商务的发展

过去，人们喜欢去商店、市场、超市和商城购物。当我们购物时，要亲自去那些地方。后来，人们有了新的购物方式，比如邮购、电视购物、电话购物等。我们购买的商品将被送到我们指定的地点。近几年来，互联网已经在以一种难以置信的速度发展，人们开始思考怎样在互联网上没有实体店铺地销售商品。举例来说，像一些著名的公司比如亚马逊、戴尔，它们起步时就开始在网络上向消费者销售它们的产品。它们已经在电子商务方面获得了巨大的成功！这种销售模式被称为 B2C（企业对个人），类似于网络零售。

通过互联网做生意被称为"电子商务"，它日益被越来越多的人所接受，特别是受过良好教育的年轻人。当非典在中国发生时，许多原本计划到访广交会的外国买家改变想法，开始用在线向中国供应商网上采购的方式代替亲自来华采购。当时，阿里巴巴获得了长足的进步，并被越来越多的企业所接受。阿里巴巴为买卖双方提供了一个互相搜寻各自感兴趣的商品并达成交易的平台。这种模式被称为 B2B（企业对企业），类似于网络批发。同时，淘宝提供了一个个人买卖的平台，这种模式被称为 C2C（个人对个人），类似于消费者之间的零售。

随着互联网的普及，我们相信电子商务将比以往发展得更快。

泛读

## 网上支付

不同于传统购物，买方不可以面对面地付款给卖方。因此网络购物以网上银行来完成付款，依赖第三方网上支付平台来保障安全。网上银行是将消费者的终端通过互联网与银行终端相连，以实现银行的服务延伸至消费者的办公室或家庭，使得消费者足不出户就可以管理自己的账户而不受银行营业时间的限制。

到目前为止，许多商业银行都已经开通了网银服务。这给在网上购物的人们带来了便利，他们可以在家里进行账户查询、转账和支付贷款等操作。但是在使用这项服务之前，你必须申请开通服务。通常，在许多银行的主页上，他们都提供网上银行业务的链接。

为了安全地使用网上银行服务，我们不得不总是保持警惕，尽管银行已经提供了某些安全措施。如果你的电脑受到了一些特洛伊木马病毒的侵害，你的银行账户和密码可能被盗，到那时就可能产生损失。

支付宝是由阿里巴巴集团提供的第三方服务，它可以帮助保护在阿里巴巴和淘宝上买卖双方的付款安全。流程如下：买方在线订购、买方付款保障、卖方发运货物、买方确认收货，卖方收款。如今，支付宝是中国最受欢迎的在线支付系统，成功地解决了买卖双方之间的信任问题。

相关链接

**只在中国：麦当劳进入在线销售消费品**
（来源：2009年4月28日，华尔街日报，引自中国日报）

2009年2月，麦当劳在中国领先的拍卖网站——阿里巴巴旗下的淘宝网上推出了一个网上商店，为其超值套餐进行促销。不过，这家快餐巨头并没有在网店上销售汉堡。在两个月的时间内，麦当劳在网上销售的是手机、数码相机和MP3播放器等流行时尚产品，还有更为意料之内的现金券。很多礼券都是以促销的折扣价出售的。

麦当劳中国首席市场营销官张家茵表示，麦当劳天天超值店是公司推出的第一家网络商店。她说，这是针对合适受众所采取的战略媒体策略；具体来说，就是对准了20多岁的都市年轻人。

其他主要的品牌，如宝洁、戴尔、联想和三星等重要品牌已经在淘宝上开设了网店。中国主要电视机生产商创维和大型IT产品分销商神州数码则与百度旗下的有啊网合作推出了网络业务。日本主要服装零售商Fast Retailing Co.旗下的休闲服装品牌优衣库近期也宣布推出类似举措。优衣库上周宣布与淘宝合作推出一家虚拟旗舰店。

麦当劳还借助一个拍卖系统来促销其超值套餐。麦当劳在淘宝网店上以接近零售价的价格推出电子产品，但用户单击的时候则会降价。第一个出到16.5元(超值套餐的价格，约合2.50美元)的淘宝用户则以这个价格拍到该商品。

麦当劳已经将中国定为重要增长市场。目前麦当劳在中国运营着1000多家餐厅，并计划今年再新开大约150家餐厅。今年早些时候，麦当劳还将大约四成的产品进行了降价，最大降幅达到了1/3。

**中国东方航空与阿里巴巴在电子商务领域结成战略联盟**
（来源：http://www.abnnewswire.net）

上海，2009年11月24日(亚洲财经新闻)中国东方航空，中国领先的航空承运商，已经和阿里巴巴集团的支付宝和淘宝两家子公司建立战略联盟，以通过电子商务来拓展东方航空服务更多消费者的能力。在这个联盟中，支付宝将对中国东方航空网站(www.ceair.com)门票销售的在线支付提供支持。中国东方航空则将在淘宝商城推出一家旗舰店，直接向顾客销售国内所有航线的机票。

"直接在线销售既经济又方便，从而使其成为现代化航空承运人回馈客户的最理想的一种方式。"中国东方航空公司总经理马叙伦说。"通过电子商务，中国东方旨在提高其直接门票销售比例，从而确保其在市场上的竞争优势。更多的在线销售渠道和网上支付方式将帮助公司节省运营成本、提高资本投资效率。"

"支付宝为能向中国东方航空的网站提供安全的第三方在线支付支持深感骄傲。同时它也对其在淘宝商城上的在线旗舰店提供支持。"支付宝总裁邵晓锋补充说,"由于世界各地越来越多的公司寻求通过电子商务实现对中国消费者的销售,支付宝要优先考虑继续为在线支付交易提供安全和保障设立行业标准。"

"随着越来越多的中国消费者转向淘宝来满足其生活需要,淘宝商城持续提高其供应优质产品的范围很重要。"淘宝网总裁陆兆禧说,"通过淘宝商城的中国东方航空网店,中国消费者,其中包括超过1.45亿淘宝注册用户,将有机会获得最有竞争力的机票价格,并从一个在每个购物阶段都可以托付自己需求的顾客集中服务门户网站获利。"

这个联盟突出了跨国公司转向电子商务,向现有客户提供更多便利、扩展其客户基础的宏观趋势。中国东方航空公司是许多转向淘宝商城和支付宝来发展业务、更好地为全中国客户服务的大公司中最新的一家。淘宝商城于2008年4月向淘宝用户推出旨在让他们有更多选择的企业零售商B2C平台。中国东方航空如同众多国际和国内知名品牌,如优衣库、宝洁、绫致、联想等,推出了淘宝商城在线旗舰零售店铺,依靠支付宝实现便利的网上支付。

练习一　（略）
练习二　Alibaba、eBay、Taobao、Paipai、Amazon
练习三　ICBC、CCB、ABC、CITI BANK、HSBC
练习四　1. C　2. D　3. B　4. C　5. A　6. B　7. A　8. C　9. D　10. B

# Unit Three

## Online Payment

Blog: I Can Make It Now!

Intensive Reading: Logistics

Extensive Reading: International Trade through E-commerce

Related Links: PayPal

## *I Can Make It Now!*

To my surprise, I can easily find some payments to buy the book in www.dangdang.com, because I can easily read and understand the **direction** written in Chinese.

Though dangdang.com accepts many types of payments, after I **compare** the **available** payments' **advantages and disadvantages**, I still think to **store** some money into my **Alipay account** then **transfer** the payment to dangdang is the safest way. Because I think Alipay is the biggest **third-party payment system**, if I am not satisfied with the commodity, I can have the money **refunded** through Alipay.

So I decide to **deposit** RMB35.00 into my Alipay account by **CCB E-banking**, then transfer the money to dangdang by Alipay as my payment **mode**. At last, the system **prompts** me to **confirm** and **submit** my **order**. When I finish the order and the payment, I also make

[1] **direction**: [diˈrekʃən] *n.* 方向，指导，用法说明

[2] **compare**: [kəmˈpɛə] *v.* 比较
[3] **available**: [əˈveiləbl] *adj.* 可用的
[4] **advantages and disadvantages**: 利弊得失
[5] **store**: [stɔ:] *v.* 存储、存入
[6] **Alipay account**: 支付宝账户
[7] **transfer**: [trænsˈfə:] *v.* 转账
[8] **third-party payment system**: 第三方支付系统
[9] **refunded**: 退款
[10] **deposit**: [diˈpɔzit] *v.* 存入
[11] **CCB E-banking**: 中国建设银行网上银行
[12] **mode**: [məud] *n.* 方式，模式
[13] **prompts**: prompt [prɔmpt] 的第三人称单数形式，*v.* 提示
[14] **confirm**: [kənˈfə:m] *v.* 确认
[15] **submit**: [səbˈmit] *v.* 呈送，递交
[16] **order**: [ˈɔ:də] *n.* 订单

some notes for the **above-mentioned** information in my notebook.

**Time passes as an arrow**! One morning is finished and I've spent the whole morning on the Net. It's almost 12:00 noon, I think I should close the computer and leave the afternoon for my study.

But will the book I ordered reach me on time? I've never tried online shopping, I haven't seen anybody in the bookstore, will they keep their **promise** and realize it? Dangdang is located in Beijing, and it's so far from Wenzhou. How long do I need to wait for it? Really 3 **working days** later I can receive it as they promised? Will the book really reach me next Wednesday? I'm **full of doubts**. Do you believe I can make it? Guess what will happen? Let's **wait and see**!

We have a half day off on Wednesday afternoon, I back to my dormitory after lunch. When I pass the corridor, the dorm keeper tells me there's something received for me. I'm astonished to see a **parcel marked** with my name as the **receiver**. Oh, I get the book "Big Data: A Revolution That Will Transform How We Live, Work and Think" from dangdang just the time **as expected**! I look at the parcel carefully and open it eagerly. It's sent to me **promptly**. I look at it very carefully, it's what I **am eager for**! I can't believe it but it's true!

---

[1] **above-mentioned**: [ə,bʌv'menʃənd] *adj.* 上述的

[2] **Time passes as an arrow**: 光阴似箭

[3] **promise**: ['prɔmis] *n.* 诺言

[4] **working days**: 工作日

[5] **full of doubts**: 充满疑惑

[6] **wait and see**: 等着瞧

[7] **parcel**: ['pɑ:sl] *n.* 包裹

[8] **marked**: mark [mɑ:k] 的过去分词形式，*v.* 记号

[9] **receiver**: [ri'si:və] *n.* 接收者

[10] **as expected**: 和预料的一样

[11] **promptly**: [prɔmptli] *adv.* 迅速地

[12] **be eager for**: 渴望

I can't wait to tell my parents how I've **made it**, but my parents fail to understand how I could have bought the book without going out. I open my computer and connect it to the Internet as soon as I **rush into** my own room. I want to share my first online shopping experience with all my friends by QQ and WeChat. I'd like to tell all of them that I can shop at home now! E-commerce is so marvelous to change our life little by little!

[1] **made it**：做到

[2] **rush into**：冲进

### Exercises 1:

Speaking: Express the advantages and disadvantages of online shopping in English (50~80 words).

Writing: Write down some English sayings and try to translate them into Chinese (50~80 words).

## Notes

(1) direction  说明，指示，动词形式为 direct。
(2) compare  比较，名词形式为 comparison。
(3) advantages and disadvantages  优劣，dis 是反义前缀。
(4) store  存储，商店(与 shop 同义)。
(5) RMB 即 Renminbi  人民币。
(6) CCB  中国建设银行(China Construction Bank)。
(7) mode  模式。
(8) prompt  提示。
(9) confirm  确认，名词形式为 confirmation。
(10) submit  提交，名词形式为 submission。
(11) order  命令、顺序、定购。
(12) above-mentioned  上述。
(13) time passes as an arrow  光阴似箭(谚语)。
(14) promise  承诺。
(15) locate  位于，名词形式为 location。
(16) working days  工作日。
(17) full of doubts  充满怀疑。
(18) wait and see  等着瞧。
(19) parcel  邮件，邮包。

(20) marked 是定语从句 "Which is marked" 的省略，被标出的。
(21) receiver  收件者。
(22) as expected  如期，如期望的那样。
(23) promptly  迅速地，及时地。
(24) be eager for  渴望。
(25) make it  办得到、做得到。
(26) rush into  冲入。

## Tips for Translation

(1) 当翻译英语中的"direction"等以"tion"结尾的词汇时，可以采用举一反三的方法借以扩充自己的词汇量。如"direct"是表示"指导、指示"的动词，"direction"自然是表示上述动作的名词，而"director"则表示作出指示的人，如"负责人、导演"等。电影字幕中常见的"Directed by"表示"由某人导演"。

(2) "available"表示"可得到的、可获得的"，是一个形容词；"availability"表示"可用性、有效性、实用性"。一般以"able"结尾的单词都为形容词，以"lity"结尾都为名词。

(3) "advantage(优势)"和"disadvantage(劣势)"互为反义词，"possible(可能的)"和"impossible(不可能的)"互为反义词，"regular(规则的)"和"irregular(不规则的)"互为反义词。"dis""im""ir"等前缀均为反义前缀，但不改变词性。

(4) "confirmation"是"confirm"的名词形式，"submission"是"submit"的名词形式，可见"tion、sion"等后缀均为名词性后缀，并具有普遍性。

(5) 在将英语谚语翻译成汉语时，要尽可能在汉语中找到相近的谚语，以谚语对应谚语的翻译为最佳选择。如"Rome was not built in one day"直接翻译成"罗马并非一日建"，这显然不是最佳翻译。考虑到本谚语在英语中是表示"伟大的事业不是短期可以完成的"，我们可以用汉语中的"冰冻三尺非一日之寒"来翻译。也就是用"意译"来代替"直译"，如本例无一词直译而来，反而能更精确地表达原意。

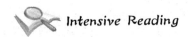
## Intensive Reading

### Logistics

**Logistics** is the name for a subject for **military** use in history. Later, logistics became a serving department for US Army. With the development of its effects, it became a new business.

For instance, you want to ship your goods from Shanghai to New York **ASAP**, the best way you may choose is to go by air. But it's impossible for you to **charter** one flight to do it, and pay its return expense. Then one Logistics company will appear to **gather** many goods to charter one flight; at the same time, he will do the same in New York for the flight back to Shanghai. In this way, you only need to pay a **reasonable** price to ship your goods, the airlines company gets more goods to earn **profits**, and logistics companies also get something they want. Many logistics companies **originate** from **express** companies, they **deliver** documents and parcels first, later they extend their business for goods delivery also, with the networks they have already built before.

[1] **Logistics**：[ləu'dʒistiks] n. 物流
[2] **military**：['militəri] n. 军队
[3] **ASAP**：abbr. 越快越好（As Soon As Possible 的缩写）
[4] **charter**：['tʃɑ:tə] v. 包租
[5] **gather**：['gæðə] v. 聚集
[6] **reasonable**：['ri:znəbl] adj. 合理的
[7] **profits**：n. 利润
[8] **originate**：[ə'ridʒineit] v. 开始
[9] **express**：[iks'pres] n. 快递
[10] **deliver**：[di'livə] v. 递送

For E-commerce, buyers usually doesn't know the sellers, even they can never see each other. The **transportation** for the goods they trade is usually done by logistics companies, because it's very **economical**. And even sometimes the logistics company will get the payment from buyers for sellers after buyers see the goods when they are delivering them. Of course they can earn some **handling charge**. In this way, buyers pay money safer, sellers receive money safer, finally the E-commerce is done more **smoothly**.

"If my client can finish the logistics himself at a cost, he will not ask me to do it at a cost of one more penny", a famous person in logistics line said. Now, more and more logistics company are competing in Chinese market, such as Fedex, DHL, TNT, UPS, also STO, YTO, TTKD, SFEXPRESS and etc.. Anyway, the more logistics companies exist, the faster E-commerce develop.

[1] **transportation**：[ˌtrænspɔːˈteiʃən] *n.* 运输

[2] **economical**：[ˌiːkəˈnɔmikəl] *adj.* 经济的

[3] **handling**：[ˈhændliŋ] *n.* 处理
[4] **charge**：[tʃɑːdʒ] *n.* 费用

[5] **smoothly**：[ˈsmuːðli] *adv.* 流畅地

### Exercise 2：

List at least 3 E-commerce types in English.

## Notes

(1) logistics 物流,起源于美国,原为军事后勤学的意思,后含义扩展为物资流动的科学合理安排,现主要指安排货物合理运输的行业。

(2) ASAP 越快越好 As Soon As Possible,也有 asap 或 a.s.a.p.等表示方法,多见于信件、邀请函等。更为客气的表述是 at your earliest convenience,意为"在您尽早方便的时刻"。以上两种表达法是英语书信中非常常见的固定用法。

(3) charter 特许,被特许的是 chartered。如著名的英国渣打银行英文名称为 Chartered Bank,因为渣打银行是于 1853 年在维多利亚女皇的特许(中文音译为"渣打")下建立的。现名为标准渣打银行,Standard Chartered Bank。

(4) gather 聚集,经常用其名词形式 gathering 表示聚会等意,与 together(一起)属于同一字根。

(5) reasonable 合理的,其反义词形式为 unreasonable,由 "un+reason+able",able 后缀的作用是将名词形容词化,而 un 前缀的作用是将形容词反义化。

(6) profits 利润,其形容词 profitable 表示有利润的,盈利的,常见于商务英语。

(7) originate 开始,其形容词形式 original 表示原始的,起源的;同时 original 也可做名词用,在商务英语中表示原件、正本等含义。

(8) express 快递,目前许多公司均用该词表示快递、快运等含义。如美国著名的快递公司联邦快递 Fedex,即由 "Federal+express"复合而来。

(9) deliver 递送,其名词形式 delivery,形容词形式 delivered,常见于物流英语中,表示货物已处于递送状态。

(10) economical 经济的、实惠的,该词同一字根的词很多,如 economy 经济,economics 经济学,economist 经济学家,而 economic 经济(学)表示的是经济方面的,不同于 economical 经济实惠的。

(11) charge 费用,也可做动词,表示收费。如 How much will you charge me? 你向我收多少费?最常见的词组是 free of charge 免费,与 complimentary(赠送的)相当。

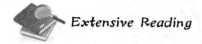 **Extensive Reading**

## International Trade through E-commerce

International trade is the trade made between two different countries or regions. Because it's more difficult and **complicated** than **domestic** trade, people need to learn more skills before they start than they do with the latter. It's more convenient for buyers and sellers to know and see each other in domestic trade than in international trade. For example, if one buyer is **doubting** about one seller's credit in domestic trade, he can **inquire** about it easily at very low cost. But in international trade, he has to spend more time and energy at much higher cost to make it. On the contrary, if international trade can be done through E-commerce, more cost will be **saved** than domestic trade can. In international trade through E-commerce, people can save a lot of expenses for flights and **accommodations**, and time as well. Besides, people usually choose their business **partners** face to face in international trade fairs in the beginning, and different **trade fairs** only aim at different **target regional markets**.

[1] **complicated**:['kɔmplikeitid] *adj.* 复杂的
[2] **domestic**:[də'mestik] *adj.* 国内的

[3] **doubting**:['dautiŋ] *adj.* 有疑心的

[4] **inquire**:[in'kwaiə] *v.* 询问

[5] **saved**:save 的过去分词形式，*v.* 节约

[6] **accommodations**：accommodation [əkɔmə'deiʃən] 的复数，*n.* 居住设施，膳宿
[7] **partners**：partner ['pɑ:tnə] 的复数，*n.* 搭档，伙伴
[8] **trade fairs**：商品交易会
[9] **target**:['tɑ:git] *n.* 靶，目标
[10] **regional markets**：区域性市场

[1] **territorial restrictions**：区域限制

[2] **Undoubtedly**：[ʌnˈdautidli] adv. 无疑地

[3] **two parties**：双方

But when people choose business partners through E-commerce, they can aim at the markets all over the world without **territorial restrictions**. It means to choose more markets and partners at lower cost. With the development of E-commerce, more and more people prefer to do international trade on line. **Undoubtedly**, Internet will affect international trade very much and help the **two parties** save a lot of cost. So, we think international trade through E-commerce will have a brighter future tomorrow!

 Exercise 3:

List at least 5 regions from the major trade partners of China.

For example: The United States of America.

 Related Links

## PayPal

(Source: https://www.paypal.com)

**PayPal** is the faster, safer way to pay and get paid **online**. The service allows members to send money without sharing **financial information**, with the **flexibility** to pay using their **account balances**, bank accounts, credit cards or promotional financing. With more than 100 million active accounts in 190 markets and 24 **currencies** around the world, PayPal enables global E-commerce. PayPal is an eBay company and is made up of three leading online payment services: the PayPal global payments platform, the Payflow **Gateway** and Bill Me Later.

PayPal is an E-commerce business allowing payments and money **transfers** to be made through the Internet. PayPal serves as an electronic **alternative** to traditional paper methods such as checks and money orders.

A PayPal account can be **funded** with an electronic debit from a bank account or by a **credit card**. The **recipient** of a PayPal transfer can either request a check from PayPal, establish their own PayPal **deposit** account or request a transfer to their bank account. PayPal is an example of a payment **intermediary** service that **facilitates** worldwide E-commerce.

PayPal performs payment processing for online **vendors**, **auction sites**, and other commercial users, for which it **charges** a fee. It sometimes also charges a

[1] **PayPal**：['peipəl] n. 贝宝
[2] **online**：['ɔnlain] adj. 联机的，在线的
[3] **financial information**：金融信息
[4] **flexibility**：[,fleksə'biliti] n. 灵活性
[5] **account balances**：账户余款
[6] **currencies**：currency ['kʌrənsi] 的复数，n. 货币
[7] **Gateway**：['geitwei] n. 门，通路
[8] **transfers**：n. 传输
[9] **alternative**：[ɔ:l'tə:nətiv] n. 替换物
[10] **funded**：fund [fʌnd] 的过去分词形式，v. 提供资金，充值
[11] **credit card**：n. 信用卡
[12] **recipient**：[ri'sipiənt] n. 接受者
[13] **deposit**：[di'pɔzit] n. 存款
[14] **intermediary**：[,intə'mi:diəri] n. 仲裁者，调解者，媒介物，中间状态
[15] **facilitates**：facilitate [fə'siliteit] 的第三人称单数形式，v. 帮助，使……容易，促进
[16] **vendors**：vendor ['vendɔ:] 的复数，n. 厂商
[17] **auction**：['ɔ:kʃən] n. 拍卖
[18] **sites**：site [sait] 的复数，n. 位置，网站
[19] **charges**：v. 索取费用

[1] **transaction**：[træn'zækʃən] *n.* 交易，处理

[2] **subsidiary**：[səb'sidiəri] *n.* 子公司

[3] **significant**：[sig'nifikənt] *adj.* 重要的，有意义的

[4] **China UnionPay**：中国银联

**transaction** fee for receiving money(a percentage of the amount sent plus an additional fixed amount). The fees charged depend on the currency used, the payment option used, the country of the sender, the country of the recipient, the amount sent and the recipient's account type. In addition, eBay purchases made by credit card through PayPal may incur a "foreign transaction fee" if the seller is located in another country, as credit card issuers are automatically informed of the seller's country of origin.

On October 3, 2002, PayPal became a wholly owned **subsidiary** of eBay. Its corporate headquarters are in San José, California, United States at eBay's North First Street satellite office campus. The company also has **significant** operations in Omaha, Nebraska; Scottsdale, Arizona; and Austin, Texas in the U.S., Chennai, Dublin, Berlin and Tel-Aviv. As of July 2007, across Europe, PayPal also operates as a Luxembourg-based bank.

On March 17, 2010, PayPal entered into an agreement with **China UnionPay**(CUP), China's bankcard association, to allow Chinese consumers to use PayPal to shop online.

## Exercise 4：

Translate the following English words or expressions into Chinese.

1. node
2. in-house program
3. credit card
4. vertical market
5. negotiation
6. particular file format
7. web page
8. spending analysis
9. desktop
10. key issues
11. B2B
12. market niche
13. broadband
14. on-line payment
15. net loss

## 参考译文及答案

# 单元三

博客

### 我会网购了

令我惊奇的是,我很容易地就在当当网上找到了许多购书的支付方式,因为我很容易理解中文的操作指示。

尽管当当网接受许多不同的支付方式,我比较了各种可能的支付方式的利弊以后,我依然认为支付宝是在当当网购物最安全的付款方式。因为我觉得支付宝是国内最大的第三方支付平台,如果我对商品不满意,可以方便地通过支付宝申请退款。

因此,我决定用我的建行网银系统将35块人民币存入支付宝账户,然后将这些钱转给当当。最后,系统迅速提示我确认和提交我的订单表格。我把上述信息记在了我的笔记本里。

时光飞逝!一个早上很快就过去了,我已经在网上度过了整个早上。现在是中午12点,我想我应该把电脑关了,把下午用来学习。但是我订购的书什么时候才能按时到我手里呢?我以前从未在网上买过东西,他们会守信并履行承诺吗?当当在北京,离温州很远。我要等多久呢?我真的可以在三天后像他们承诺的那样收到货物吗?这本书真的可以在下周三到我手中吗?我充满了疑惑。你相信我能做到吗?猜猜将会发生什么?让我们等着瞧吧!

我们星期三下午没课,午饭后我回到宿舍。当我经过走廊时,宿舍管理员叫我去拿东西。我惊喜地看到有个寄给我的包裹。哦,我就在预期的时间内收到了当当寄出的《大数据时代:生活、工作与思维的大变革》!我仔细地看着包裹,急切地打开了它。这书这么快就到了我手中。我仔细地看了又看,这就是我急切想得到的啊!我都不敢相信这是真的!

我迫不及待地告诉了我的父母我能在网上买东西了,但是他们不能理解我没有出去又是怎样买到书的?我一冲进房间就打开电脑,连上网络,我想通过QQ和微信与我的所有朋友分享我的初次网络购物经历。我要告诉他们我可以在家里购物了!电子商务是如此神奇,一点一点地改变我们的生活!

精读

### 物流

物流在历史上是用于军事方面的一个学科的名称。后来,物流成为美国军队的一个服务部门。随着作用的发挥,它成为一门生意。

例如,你想把你的货物从上海尽快运到纽约,你可能选择的最佳方法就是空运。但是你不可能租下一个航班,并支付其回程的费用。而一家物流公司会集合许多货物来租下一个航班;与此同时,他同样会在纽约为回程航班揽货。通过这样的方法,你只需要支付一个合理的价格来发运你的货物,航空公司获得更多的货物来赚取利润,物流公司也得到了他们想要的利润。许多物流公司都是从快递公司发展而来的,他们发运文件和包裹,后来拓展到货物,同样使用先前发展起来的网络。

对于电子商务而言，买方通常不认识卖方，甚至永远也不会见面。他们之间买卖货物的运输通常是通过物流公司完成的，因为这样做更经济。甚至有的物流公司还会在送货时代卖方向买方收取货款。当然，他们要赚取一些手续费。通过这样的方式，买方更安全地付款，卖方更安全地收款，最终电子商务进行得更加顺畅。

"如果我的客户以一定的成本可以自行完成物流，他不会多付一分钱让我去做。"物流业一位著名人士曾经这样说过。如今，越来越多的物流公司在中国市场上竞争，比如联邦快递、DHL、TNT、UPS，还有申通快递、圆通快递、天天快递和顺丰快递等。不管怎样，物流公司越多，电子商务就发展越快。

泛读

### 通过电子商务做国际贸易

国际贸易是在两个不同的国家或地区间进行的贸易。因为它比国内贸易更加困难和复杂，所以人们在开始做国际贸易时，较之做国内贸易需要学习更多的技巧。国内贸易的买卖双方互相认识和见面要比国际贸易的买卖双方更容易。举例来说，如果国内贸易中的一位买家怀疑一位卖家的信用，他可以用非常低的成本来询问。但是在国际贸易中，买家就需要花费更多的时间和精力，以更高的成本去实现它。相反地，如果国际贸易可以通过电子商务来做，它节省的成本就比国内贸易要多，人们可以节省大量的航班和食宿费用，也可以节省时间。此外，国际贸易中，人们最初通常选择国际贸易展会面对面地选择商业伙伴，而且不同的贸易展会只能针对不同的地区目标市场。但是当人们通过电子商务选择商业伙伴时，他们可以毫无地域限制地针对全世界的市场。这意味着以更低的成本寻找更多的市场和伙伴。随着电子商务的发展，越来越多的人倾向于在线国际贸易。毫无疑问，互联网将极大地影响国际贸易，帮助双方节省费用。因此，我们认为通过电子商务的国际贸易将会有一个更加光明的明天！

相关链接

### 贝宝
（来源：https://www.paypal.com）

贝宝提供更迅速、安全的网上支付和收款方式。会员在发送款项时无需向商家提供任何敏感的金融信息；它提供灵活的支付方式，既可使用账户余额付款，银行转账，也可用信用卡或者分期付款。贝宝在全球拥有超过1亿活跃用户，覆盖了190个市场，并支持24种货币。贝宝是易贝的一家子公司，主要有三大支柱业务：贝宝全球支付平台、Payflow支付门户和Bill me later支付平台。

贝宝的电子商务业务提供网络支付和资金转账。与传统通过纸质票据支付类似，如支票和汇票，贝宝提供的是电子化的支付方式。

贝宝账户可以用银行发行的电子借贷卡或者信用卡来充值。贝宝的收款方可以向贝宝要求支票，建立私人存款账户，或者转到他们的银行卡上。贝宝提供的是典型的即时到账服务，很大程度上推动了世界电子商务的发展。

贝宝为在线卖家、拍卖网站，还有其他商业用户提供支付服务，并收取服务费。它也对收到的款项收取一定的交易费（收到金额的一定比例加上固定的收费）。收费多少取决于所使用的货币、支付方式、发送方所在的国家、收款方所在的国家、发送的金额多少以及收款方的账户类型。另外,易贝买家使用信用卡通过贝宝支付给在他国的卖家的话,会产生"国外交易费",因为信用卡发行商会自动通知买方的所在地。

2002年10月3日,贝宝成为易贝旗下的全资子公司。它的总部在美国加利福尼亚的圣何塞,易贝所在的第一北大街的卫星易贝办公园区。公司还在多个地区设有基地,包括美国内布拉斯加州的奥马哈、亚利桑那州的斯考奇戴尔,以及得克萨斯州的奥斯汀、印度金奈、都柏林、柏林和特拉维夫。到2007年,贝宝在欧洲运营以卢森堡为基地的银行。

2010年3月17日,贝宝与中国银联(CUP)签订协议,中国用户可以使用贝宝进行网上支付。

练习一　（略）
练习二　B2C、B2B、C2C
练习三　EU、USA、Japan、Brazil、Australia
练习四　1. 节点　　　　2. 自用程序　　　3. 信用卡　　　4. 垂直市场,纵向市场
　　　　5. 谈判,协商　　6. 特殊文件格式　　　　　　　　7. 网页
　　　　8. 消费分析　　9. 桌面　　　　10. 关键问题　　11. 企业对企业
　　　　12. 市场定位　　13. 宽带　　　　14. 在线支付　　15. 净损失,净亏损

# Unit Four

## Web Design

Blog: Learning Web Design

Intensive Reading: The Structure of an HTML Page

Extensive Reading: Web Layout Basics

Related Links: Adobe

## Learning Web Design

Hello, everybody! I am Lisa Lee. Recently I have been learning **web design**. It is very interesting, because I can try to build my own web pages. Do you have interest in this? Please follow me to get some **basics** on web design.

Web design is an important part of E-commerce. You can **release** information, do shopping and make payments on web pages. And some well-designed web sites can make better sales of your products, though it is not easy.

The **original** web pages are plain text mode. Along with **appearance** of **multimedia** web, web design has become more **complex**. So you need to try your best. As to web design, you should choose a proper web editing software, such as Dreamweaver, Frontpage and etc.. Dreamweaver is a kind of software with strong **functions** and easy to learn. I **recommend** it!

Web design shares the same elements with **print design**. You need to explore the space and **layout**, handle **fonts** and colors, and put them all together.

There are five basic **elements** of web design: Line, Font, Color, **Graphic** and **Navigation**.

[1] **web design**：网页设计

[2] **basics**：basic ['beisik] 的复数，*n.* 基本知识，基本原理

[3] **release**：[ri'li:s] *v.* 释放，发布

[4] **original**：[ə'ridʒənl] *adj.* 原来的，起初的

[5] **appearance**：[ə'pirəns] *n.* 出现

[6] **multimedia**：['mʌlti'mi:djə] *adj.* 多媒体的

[7] **complex**：['kɔmpleks] *adj.* 复杂的

[8] **functions**：function ['fʌŋkʃən] 的复数，*n.* 功能，作用

[9] **recommend**：['rekə'mend] *v.* 推荐，介绍

[10] **print design**：印刷设计

[11] **layout**：['leiaut] *n.* 布局

[12] **fonts**：font [fant] 的复数，*n.* 字型，字体

[13] **elements**：element ['elimənt] 的复数，*n.* 要素，元素

[14] **Graphic**：['græfik] *n.* 图形

[15] **Navigation**：[,nævi'geiʃən] *n.* 导航

[1] **borders:** border ['bɔ:də] 的复数,
n. 边界

[2] **vertical:** ['və:tikəl] adj. 竖的, 垂直的

[3] **horizontal:** ['hɔri'zɔntəl] adj. 水平的

[4] **delineate:** [di'linieit] v. 描绘, 刻画

[5] **tag:** [tæg] n. 标签, 标记

[6] **family:** 此处译为"语族"

[7] **typography:** [tai'pɔgrəfi] n. 印刷术, 排印工艺, 排字[同义]printing

[8] **precise:** [pri'sais] adj. 准确的, 精确的

[9] **hexadecimal:** ['heksə,desiməl] adj. 十六进制(法)的

[10] **render:** ['rendə] v. 着色, 此处译为"识别"

Lines include **borders** and rules. They can be **vertical** or **horizontal** and help **delineate** the spaces around elements on web pages.

Fonts are the way your text looks on a web page. And most web pages have large amounts of text. As a beginner, you should not put all the words in a web page. I've once made a long web page. Unfortunately it was easy to get lost during reading.

If you have been writing HTML for a while, you've probably come across the <font> **tag**. This is an old tag that allows you to set the font size, color and **family**. Luckily Cascading Style Sheets (CSS) allow you to make your web **typography** very **precise** and your fonts will never be the same.

When you're starting to build your web page, keep in mind that color is a kind of useful design element. Color can be used in tables, as backgrounds, and fonts, it can make your web page much more interesting and beautiful. The visitors will love it at first sight.

There are different ways of adding color to your pages. One is using the named colors. But it's better to use **hexadecimal** codes for your color names, because some browsers don't **render** color names. The other way is using CCS.

Graphics are the fun part of most web pages. As the saying goes "a picture is worth 1000 words" and that's also true in web design. Nearly every web page has some photos on it, and a photo can do more to improve your pages. People won't buy the product if they can't see it. If you can, take photos of the product from **multiple** sides. This gives your customers more information.

On the other hand, if you have a bad photo or image on your page, you can damage your site's **credibility** and lose customers and sales.

Navigation is how the visitors get around from one page to another on a web site. Navigation provides movement and gives the chance to find other elements of your site. You need to make sure that the structure of your web site makes sense, so that the visitors aren't **confused**.

Some common elements on a business web page are:

Products—the products or services the company sells

About—information about the company

Support—help for customers

Talent—talent on demand

In addition, web design also includes HTML, web layout, web **database** and etc.. Please follow me again.

[1] **multiple**：['mʌltəpl] *adj.* 数量多的，多样的

[2] **credibility**：[ˌkredi'biliti] *n.* 信誉，可信度

[3] **confused**：[kən'fju:zd] *adj.* 困惑的，糊涂的

[4] **database**：['deitəbeis] *n.* 数据库

## Exercises 1:

Choose the best option and fill in the bracket with the mark No..

1. The multimedia web page often contains (　　).
   A. texts                B. images
   C. videos               D. audio files        E. all of the above

2. Which one is not the basic elements of web design? (　　)
   A. lines                B. fonts
   C. images               D. colors             E. width

3. In web pages, color can be used (　　).
   A. in tables            B. in fonts
   C. as backgrounds       D. all of the above

4. The customers can get cargo information from (　　) on the web page.
   A. texts                B. images
   C. movies               D. all of the above

5. Which one is wrong about images using in web design? (　　)
   A. take photos from multiple sides
   B. delete the bad images on your page
   C. images are the fun part of a web page
   D. take as many images as you can in a web page

6. (　　) is the common taxonomy element on a business web page.
   A. Product              B. About
   C. Support              D. Talent             E. All of the above

7. Words and Phrases Learning.

| | |
|---|---|
| ① come across | when you see sb./sth. for the first time |
| ② keep in mind | from another point of view |
| ③ at first sight | to be easy to understand or explain |
| ④ on the other hand | to remember or pay attention |
| ⑤ makes sense | thing after something else |
| ⑥ in addition | to meet or find sb./sth. by chance |
| ⑦ horizontal | at the beginning of a particular period |
| ⑧ confuse | to tell sb. that sth. is good or useful |
| ⑨ original | going across and parallel to the ground |
| ⑩ recommend | to make sb. unable to think clearly or understand something |

## Notes

(1) have interest in = be interested in  对……有兴趣。

例句：Actually, I do not have any interest in calligraphy. 实际上，我对书法不感兴趣。

I'm not interested in music. 我对音乐不感兴趣。

(2) do shopping = go shopping  (去)购物。

(3) well-designed  设计很好的；构思甚佳的。

例句：Buses in Japan are well-designed. 日本巴士设计得很好。

(4) plain texts  纯文本。

例句：Describes the differences between plain text mode and HTML in Outlook Express. 描述 Outlook Express 中纯文本模式和 HTML 模式之间的差异。

(5) along with (sb./sth.)  与……一起，随着，除……以外(还)。

例句：She came along with us. 她是同我们一起来的。

Along with the letters there are answers written by people who are supposed to know how to solve such problems. 与这些读者来信一起，还刊登对这些问题的回答，由那些被认为能够解决这些问题的人来撰写。

(6) as to  至于，关于。

例句：As to intelligence, the boy has more than he can possibly make use of. 至于那男孩的才智，多得他都用不完。

(7) share sth. with sb.  与(某人)分享(某物)。

例句：He would share his last dollar with me. 他要是剩下最后一块钱也会跟我分着用。

(8) large amounts of  大量的，与 a large amount of 同义。large amounts of 后面接可数名词，也可接不可数名词；a large amount of 后面接不可数名词。

例句：Gas bubbles in the ash left holes that store large amounts of water for plant use. 火山灰内的气泡会留下空洞，它可以储藏大量水分供植物利用。

Governments in many countries spend large amounts of resources on irrigation. 许多国家的政府在水利化方面花费了大量资金。

He borrowed a large amount of money from the bank. 他向银行借了一大笔钱。

(9) for a while  一段时间，同义词组是 a period of time。

例句：Please keep me company for a while. 陪陪我吧！

(10) come across 偶遇，碰到(偶然)，与 encounter、run across 同义。

例句：We came across an old man lying in the road. 我们碰见一位老人躺在路上。

One day I happened to run across her. 有一天我碰巧见到她了。

(11) Cascading Style Sheets (即 CSS)层叠样式表，它定义如何显示 HTML 元素，样式通常存储在样式表中，把样式添加到 HTML 4.0 中，是为了解决内容与表现分离的问题。

(12) keep…in mind 记得，记住，牢记。

例句：Please keep in mind the glory of Chicago. 请记住芝加哥的荣耀。

(13) background 出身背景，后景，背景，底色。

同类型词：backroom 密室; backhand 反手; backdoor 后门。

(14) at first sight 乍一看，初看时，初次见到。

例句：At first sight the house appeared to be empty than it really is. 乍看起来这房子似乎空无一人，但实际上并非如此。

Love at first sight 一见钟情的美丽，是澳洲女歌手 Kylie Minogue 的一首歌。

(15) hexadecimal codes (颜色的)十六进制编码。例如：

(16) as the saying goes 常言道。

例句：You have to look before you leap, as the saying goes. 俗话说，做事要三思而后行。

(17) On the other hand 在另一方面。

例句：He is a bad cook, but on the other hand, he certainly can bake a good cake. 他是一个差劲的厨子，但从另一方面来看，他的确能烘烤好吃的。

(18) get around 传播，流传，各处走动。

get round/around sth. 成功地对付，解决，克服。

get round/around sb. (用讨好的手段)说服某人同意，笼络某人。

例句：Does Abell get around a great deal? 艾贝尔常出去走动吗？

(19) make sense 有意义，讲得通，有道理。

例句：This sentence doesn't make any sense. 这个句子没有意义。

(20) talent on demand 人才需求，此处列出了企业网站常见的分类内容。

(21) web database 网络数据库。

# Tips for Translation

(1) make better sales of your products. 意为带来更好的销售。

(2) Fonts are the way your text looks on a web page. 这是一个定语从句，the way 后面省略了 that，这里的关系副词 that 在从句中不做任何成分。

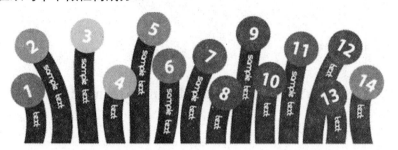

way 主要有以下 4 种用法：way to do；way of doing；way that +从句；way in which+从句。

(3) so that the visitors aren't confused. 句中 confused 是过去分词作表语(类似于形容词)。类似情况还有：The city is surrounded on three sides by mountains. 这座城市三面环山。

(4) Some common elements on a business web page are… 此处的 elements 不再指代前面的 Line, Font, Color, Graphic and Navigation，而是网站栏目(频道)的意思。

(5) Please follow me again. 此处是省略句，完整的句子是：Please follow me again to get some basics on HTML, web layout and etc..

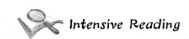

## Intensive Reading

### The Structure of an HTML Page

An HTML page is divided into two **major** sections:

1. The head

The head (<head>) section contains **underlying** information about the page which does not get **displayed** in the web page (except for the title of the page). It does, however, have an effect on how the web page is displayed.

2. The body

The body (<body>) section contains all the **stuff** that appears on the actual web page when someone happens to come along with their web browser. We are talking about the actual text, images, flash movies, and so on that people will see. That, of course, means the tags used to format all this stuff are there too...

You will notice that both the head and the body sections of a website are marked in the HTML page with their **respective** tags: (<head> </head>) and (<body> </body>).

---

[1] **major**: ['meidʒə] *adj.* 主要的，重要的，[同义]greater

[2] **underlying**: [ˌʌndə'laiiŋ] *adj.* 根本的，潜在的，隐含的

[3] **displayed**: [di'spleid] *adj.* 显示的

[4] **stuff**: [stʌf] *n.* 东西，材料，[同义]matter

[5] **respective**: [ri'spektiv] *adj.* 各自的，各个的，[同义]own

If the body tag creates the body of an HTML page, and the head tag creates the head of an HTML page, how do you create an HTML page itself? You guessed it, use the HTML tags: <html> </html>.

The **mother** of all tags' is the HTML (<html>) tag, and like all tags it must have a start tag (<html>) and an end tag (</html>). The difference between the start and end tags is the forward **slash** (/), but you already knew that.

Every web page must begin and end with the HTML tag, **otherwise** the web browser (programs like Internet Explorer) will not be able to display the page. You also have to have the head tags and the body tags. All the other tags are **optional**.

So the bare-bones HTML page must have these tags and in this order:

<html>
  <head>
    <title>Title of your page</title>
  </head>
  <body>
    This is your own web page!
  </body>
</html>

[1] **mother**：此处应译为母标记或外层标记

[2] **slash**：[slæʃ] *n.* 斜杠，斜线号

[3] **otherwise**：[ˈʌðəwaiz] *adv.* 否则，不然，除此以外

[4] **optional**：[ˈɔpʃənl] *adj.* 可自由选择的，非强制性的，[同义]discretional

### Exercise 2: Determine Title

1. The information of the head section is always visible in the page. （　）
2. The body section contains plain text information only. （　）
3. Every web page must begin and end with the HTML tag. （　）
4. Both the head and the body sections use the same HTML tags. （　）
5. The most commonly used web browser is Internet Explorer. （　）

## Notes

(1) 有些字母(如 a、e、f、h、i 等)或缩略词,若第一个音是元音,不定冠词也应用 an。

例句:He missed an "n" in the word. 他写的这个单词漏了一个"n"。

(2) divide sth. (up) (into sth.)　分开,分割,分成。

例句:Three will not divide into seven. 三除不尽七。

A sentence can be divided up into meaningful segments. 一个句子可以划分成有意义的几个部分。

(3) The head 指 HTML 文件的文件头部分,使用<head>表示文件头的开始,使用</head>表示文件头的结束,中间是文件头部分的具体内容。文件头 head 是用来包含其他标记的容器,比如可以包含 Title 和 Meta 等标记,控制页面的 JavaScript 程序和控制网页格式的 CSS 文件也放在 head 之内。

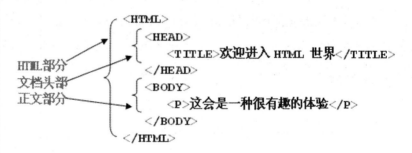

(4) have an effect on　对……有作用,对……有影响。

例句:Does television have an effect on children's behavior? 电视对孩子的行为有影响吗?

(5) The body 指 HTML 文件的文件体部分,它是一个 HTML 文档最核心的部分,用户浏览器中显示的信息都定义在 body 标记之内。它使用<body>表示文件体的开始,使用</body>表示文件体的结束。

(6) happen to　发生于,碰巧发生(某事)。

例句:I was unable to find out what had happened to him. 我无法发现他出了什么事。

(7) come along (with)　跟随，到达，出现，赶紧。

例句：I'm glad you came along. 我很高兴你跟我一起来。

Come along! We are late. 快点！我们要迟到了。

She came along with us. 她是同我们一起来的。

(8) The body (<body>) section: this section contains all the stuff... 本段话很长，结构也比较复杂，后面还追加了一些解释，因而显得较难翻译。that appears on the actual web page 是宾语从句，是对前面 stuff 的解释；when someone happens to come along with their web browser 是条件状语从句。We are talking about the actual text, images, flash movies, and so on that people will see. 这句话进一步解释了 stuff 所指代的一些具体内容，如文本、图片、动画等；That, of course, means the tags used to format all this stuff are there too... 这句话指明了 stuff 还包括用于标记网页格式的那些 html 标记。

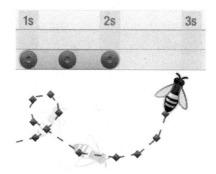

(9) begin and end with　开始和结束于……

例句：Begin with thunder and end with a drizzle. 雷声大雨点小。

A non-scan field must begin and end with address delimiters. 非扫描字段必须以地址定界符开始和结束。

(10) bare-bones　极简单的，基础的。the bare bones (of sth.)　梗概，概要。

例句：The bare bones of a story. 故事梗概。

(11) in order　整齐有序；按顺序，按次序。

例句：Everything is in order. 一切都准备好了/一切就绪。

 **Extensive Reading**

## Web Layout Basics

When people talk about web design, they first think of the layout. Layout is the **organization** of elements on a web page. First you need to start with basic design **principles**. Once you understand them, you can **master** how to place elements on your web page. The article will take you through the steps to learn good web layout design.

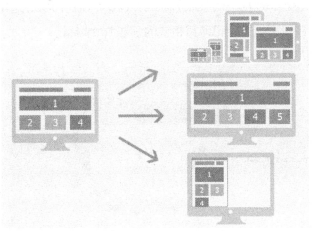

### Space and Whitespace

Use the whole space. In other words, use **relatively** sized layout sections on your web pages, so that they **expand** or **contract** to fit the browser window.

Pay attention to screen resolution. Now the majority of computer users have moved away from 800× 600 **resolution**, keep that in mind when you're designgnning.

---

[1] **organization**：[ˌɔːɡənaɪˈzeɪʃən] *n.* 组织，团体，机构

[2] **principles**：principle [ˈprɪnsəpl] 的复数，*n.* 原则，原理

[3] **master**：[ˈmɑːstə] *v.* 精通，掌握，控制

[4] **Space and Whitespace**：空白符

[5] **relatively**：[ˈrelətɪvli] *adv.* 相对地，相关地

[6] **expand**：[ɪksˈpænd] *v.* 扩大，增加，增强，[同义]extend, enlarge

[7] **contract**：[ˈkɔntrækt] *v.* 缩小

[8] **resolution**：[ˌrezəˈluːʃən] *n.* 分辨率

Use color to define spaces

If you want to have a page that's a specific **width**, why not center it on the browser screen and make the background color of the page a different color? This will help the page appear to **resize** for different browsers.

Images and Graphics

**Align** your images. One of the most common **newbie** layout mistakes is to slap images into a page without thought to layout. Using the align **attribute** will help make your images part of the layout.

Balance the graphics and text

It's easy to get carried away with lots of images and **animations**, but they can make a page very hard to read. When you're considering your layout, remember that images are only one part of the design.

Text Width

When designing your layouts, make sure that the major text area displays the text in a readable width. Most people can comfortably read about 7 to 11 words on a line. Longer than that, and the text is hard to read, shorter than that, and it's **disjointed** and **distracting**.

Centering text is unwise. It is very difficult to do well and it's often hard to read.

[1] **width**：[widθ] *n.* 宽度

[2] **resize**：[riːsaiz] *v.* 改变（尤指计算机图像）的大小

[3] **Align**：[əˈlain] *v.* 排整齐，校准，对齐，[同义]tidy

[4] **newbie**：[njuːbi] *n.*（尤指计算机方面的）新手，[同义] novice，[反义] veteran

[5] **attribute**：[ˈætribjuːt] *n.* 特性、属性

[6] **animations**：animation [ˌæniˈmeiʃən] 的复数，*n.* 动画，动画片

[7] **disjointed**：[disˈdʒɔintid] *adj.* 杂乱的

[8] **distracting**：[diˈstræktiŋ] *adj.* 分心的

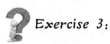 Exercise 3：

Speaking: How to balance the images and the texts in a web page?
Writing: Use your own words to summarize this article.

## Notes

(1) take…through　使通过，带……通过。

例句：Fish take in oxygen through their gills. 鱼通过鳃呼吸。

(2) in other words　换句话说。

例句：His wife is my daughter, in other words, I am his mother-in-law. 他妻子是我女儿，换句话讲，我是他的岳母。

(3) the majority of　大部分，[同义] most。

(4) move away　搬走。

例句："Do the Simpsons still live here?" "No, they've moved away." "辛普森一家还住这儿吗？""不住这儿了，他们已搬走了。"

(5) appear to　看来像是，看来似乎。

例句：It appear to have hit a rock. 这船好像触了礁石。

(6) get(be) carry away　十分激动，十分兴奋。

例句：Don't be carried away by success. 不要被胜利冲昏头脑。

(7) readable　可读性强的，通俗易懂的。

类似的复合词：capable 合适的，能干的；reliable 可靠的。

## Related Links

### *Adobe*

(Sources: http://www.adobe.com)

Adobe Systems Incorporated was founded in 1982. As a leader in Software-as-a-Service, their software and technologies have **set the standard** for communication and **collaboration** for more than 25 years, bringing **vital** and **engaging** experiences to people across media and to **every screen** in their lives, at work and at **play**.

The impact of Adobe software is **evident** almost everywhere you look. Whether people are collaborating at work, transacting online, or **socializing** with friends, businesses use Adobe software and technologies to turn digital **interactions** into richer, high value experiences that reach **across computing platforms** and devices to engage people anywhere, anytime.

With a **reputation** for excellence and a **portfolio** of many of the most respected and **recognizable** software brands, Adobe is one of the world's largest and most **diversified** software companies.

Adobe has a rich history of **innovation**, their **commitment** to innovation is as strong today as it was in 1982, when Chuck Geschke and John Warnock founded Adobe. The two men **initially** set out to solve a problem long familiar to creative professionals at the time: getting text and images on a computer screen

[1] **set the standard**：设立标准
[2] **collaboration**：[kə,læbəˈreiʃən] *n.* 合作，协作
[3] **vital**：[ˈvaitl] *adj.* 必要的，重要的
[4] **engaging**：[inˈgeidʒiŋ] *adj.* 有趣的，迷人的
[5] **every screen**：代指"每个人"
[6] **play**：娱乐
[7] **evident**：[ˈevidənt] *adj.* 显然的，明显的
[8] **socializing**：socialize [ˈsəuʃəlaiz] 的 ing 形式，*v.* 社交
[9] **interactions**：interaction [,intəˈrækʃən] 的复数，*n.* 互动
[10] **across computing platforms**：跨计算机平台

[11] **reputation**：[,repjuˈteiʃən] *n.* 名誉，名声
[12] **portfolio**：[pɔːtˈfəuljəu] *n.* 系列产品
[13] **recognizable**：[ˈrekəgnaizəbl] *adj.* 容易认出的
[14] **diversified**：[daiˈvəːsifaid] *adj.* 多样化的
[15] **innovation**：[,inəuˈveiʃən] *n.* 创新
[16] **commitment**：[kəˈmitmənt] *n.* 承诺，奉献
[17] **initially**：[iˈniʃəli] *adv.* 最初，[同义] at first, originally

[1] **accurately**: ['ækjuritli] *adv.* 准确地，精确地

[2] **launch**: [lɔ:ntʃ] *v.* 发动，发射，产生，推出

[3] **radical**: ['rædikəl] *adj.* 全新的

[4] **approach**: [ə'prəutʃ] *n.* 方法

[5] **embraced**: embrace [im'breis] 的过去式，*v.* 拥抱，接受

[6] **visionary**: ['viʒənəri] *n.* 有远见的人

[7] **insurmountable**: [,insə'mauntəbl] *adj.* 难以解决的

[8] **complexity**: [kəm'pleksiti] *n.* 复杂性

[9] **interconnected**: [,intəkə'nektid] *adj.* 连通的

[10] **emerged**: emerge [i'mə:dʒ] 的过去式，*v.* 出现，显现

[11] **Incompatible operating systems**: 不兼容的操作系统

[12] **hindered**: hinder ['hində] 的过去式，*v.* 阻碍，妨碍

[13] **skyrocketed**: skyrocket [skaiərɔkit] 的过去式，*v.* 猛涨

to translate beautifully and **accurately** into print. A year later, they helped **launch** the desktop publishing revolution with Adobe PostScript, a technology that took the publishing world by storm with its **radical** new **approach** to printing text and images.

That was just the beginning. From the earliest days, Adobe **embraced** their role as industry **visionary** and leader, continuing to solve previously **insurmountable** problems. The release of two ground breaking applications—Adobe Illustrator and Adobe Photoshop—forever changed the quality and **complexity** of images that could be created for print, and later for content created for video, film, the web and other digital channels. The design industry was never the same.

As computers became more **interconnected** and people needed to collaborate online using a wide variety of documents, a new problem **emerged**: sharing this content. **Incompatible operating systems** and programs **hindered** collaboration, a problem made worse as the use of E-mail and the web **skyrocketed**.

Adobe's **breakthrough** Portable Document Format (PDF) technology provided a solution for the problem, **enabling** businesses to deliver **platform independent** files across operating systems and devices. Suddenly, enterprises had new opportunities for document sharing and collaboration. Today, Adobe extend the benefits of **dynamic** collaboration through **web conferencing** and enterprise solutions offering powerful document security, process management, and other **capabilities**.

As the Internet **exploded** into a viable **economic engine**, Adobe quickly recognized that static HTML pages could not deliver the **end-user interactivity** and **integration** with enterprise systems that businesses required. Adobe again took the lead **first with** Adobe Dreamweaver and Flash, and later **with** Flex and the Flash Media Server by making **cost-effective**, **reliable** development of engaging websites a reality.

[1] **breakthrough**：['breik,θru:] *n.* 突破
[2] **enabling**：enable [in'eibl] 的 ing 形式，*v.* 使能够
[3] **platform independent**：平台无关的
[4] **dynamic**：[dai'næmik] *adj.* 动态的
[5] **web conferencing**：网络会议
[6] **capabilities**：capability [,keipə'biliti] 的复数，*n.* 能力，才能
[7] **exploded**：explode [iks'pləud] 的过去式，*v.* 爆炸，爆破
[8] **economic engine**：经济引擎
[9] **end-user**：终端用户
[10] **interactivity**：[intəræktivəti] *n.* 交互性
[11] **integration**：[,inti'greiʃən] *n.* 整合，集成
[12] **first with…later with**：先是……后是……
[13] **cost-effective**：成本效益好的
[14] **reliable**：[ri'laiəbl] *adj.* 可靠的

[1] **FedEx**：联邦快递
[2] **Sony Pictures**：索尼电影公司
[3] **T-Mobile**：德国电信
[4] **New York Times**：纽约时报
[5] **revenue**：['revinju:] *n.* 收入

Adobe's customers span a range of industries and represent global brands such as **FedEx**, **Sony Pictures**, **T-Mobile**, eBay and the **New York Times**. Today, more than half of Adobe's **revenue** comes from outside the United States. Adobe will deliver rich content and services for customers with the tools and technologies.

### Exercise 4: Understanding the Text

Choose the best option and fill in the bracket with the mark No..

1. Which one is not the web page editing software? (     )

   A. Dreamweaver              B. Frontpage

   C. Photoshop                D. HTML Editor

2. Which software have you ever used before? (     )

   A. Adobe reader             B. Photoshop

   C. Dreamweaver              D. Flash player

3. The main use of Adobe PostScript was (     ).

   A. collaborating at work

   B. transacting online

   C. printing images

   D. socializing with friends

4. Which one is not the product of Adobe? (     )

   A. Flex                     B. Adobe Illustrator

   C. Flash Media Server       D. RealPlayer

5. Which brand is not the Adobe's customer? (     )

   A. T-Mobile                 B. FedEx

   C. eBay                     D. Taobao

参考译文及答案

# 单元四　网页设计

博客

## 学习网页设计

大家好，我是李丽莎，最近我一直在学习网页设计，这是很有趣的内容，因为我可以建立自己的网页。对此你有兴趣吗？跟我学一些网页设计的基本知识吧！

网页设计是电子商务很重要的一部分，你可以发布信息、购物以及在线支付。一些好的网页设计可以让你的商品卖得更好，尽管这不容易。

最初的 web 网页是纯文本模式，后来多媒体网页诞生，网页设计也变得更复杂，因此你需要努力学好它。要设计网页，你首先需要选择合适的 web 编辑软件，比如 Dreamweaver、Frontpage 等。Dreamweaver 是一个功能强大而且易用的软件，我推荐你用它。

网页设计与印刷设计拥有相同的设计元素。你需要探索平面空间和布局，处理字体和颜色，并把这些元素集合在一起。

网页设计中包含 5 个基本要素：线条、字体、颜色、图片和导航。

线包括边界和规则，它们可以垂直或水平，并帮助在网页上围绕着设计元素划定特定空间。

字体是网页上的文本的显示方式。大多数网页上有大量的文字。作为初学者，你不要把所有文字放在一张网页上。我曾经制作了一个很长的页面，不幸的是在阅读中很容易失去方向。

如果你已经写了一段时间的 HTML，你可能遇到过<font>标记，<font>标记是 HTML 中的一种常用标记，使用它可以设置字体的大小、颜色和语言。幸运的是层叠样式表(CSS)可以让你的网页排版非常准确，字体的使用也将不会重复。

当你开始制作网页时，请你记住颜色是一类有用的设计元素。颜色可用于表格、背景和字体，它可以让你的网页更有趣和更美观，让读者瞬间爱上你的网页。

有很多不同的方法可以在网页上添加颜色。一种方法是使用命名的颜色，但最好使用十六进制的颜色代码，因为有些浏览器不能识别颜色名称。而使用 CSS 来添加颜色是另一种途径。

图片是所有网页上最有趣的部分。常言道："一图胜千字"，网页设计也是这样。几乎每张网页上都有图片，图片可以显著提高你的网页水平。人们不会购买自己无法看到的产品。如果可以，需要放置不同角度的产品照片，这可以给客户更多的信息。

另一方面，如果有一张糟糕的图片在你的网页上，这会损害你的网站的信誉度并且失去客户和销售额。

导航就是让访问者如何从网站上的一个网页转到另一个网页。导航提供跳转并给访问者以找到网站其他元素的机会。你需要确保你的 web 站点的结构是合理的，让访问者不会迷惑。

企业或商业网页上的常见分类内容如下。

产品——公司提供的产品或服务

关于——公司信息

支持——为客户服务

人才——人才需求

最后，网页设计还包括 HTML、网页布局、网络数据库等。请跟我继续学吧！

精读

## HTML 网页结构

一个 HTML 网页被分为以下两个主要的组成部分。

### 1. 文件头部分

文件头部分包含了有关页面的一些隐含性信息，这些信息不会显示在网页页面上(除了页面主题)。然而，它确实可以影响 web 页面是如何显示的。

### 2. 文件体部分

文件体部分包含了随用户打开 web 浏览器随之而来的，那些显示在实际页面上的所有东西，包括我们正在讨论的实际文本、图片、Flash 影片等诸如此类人们能看到的信息，这当然也包括那些用于格式化所有这些信息的标记。

你会注意到 web 网站上的头文件部分和体文件部分都被各自所使用的<head></head>和<body> </body>符号标记在了 HTML 网页上。

如果体文件标记创建了 HTML 网页的正文，头文件标记创建了 HTML 网页的头部，你如何创建一个 HTML 页面本身？你猜对了，使用 HTML 标记：<html>和</html>。

所有的 HTML 标记的上级标记是<html>标记，就像所有的标记都必须有一个开始标记<html>和一个结束标记</html>。开始标记和结束标记之间的区别在于前面的斜线号/，这你已经知道了。

每一个 web 页面必须开始和结束于这两个 HTML 标记，否则浏览器(就像 Internet Explorer 程序)将无法显示页面，你还必须使用头文件标记和体文件标记，所有其他的标记是非强制性的。

因此，一个简单的 HTML 页面必须使用那些标记，并且要符合以下次序。

```
<html>
    <head>
        <title>Title of your page</title>
    </head>
    <body>
    </body>
</html>
```

泛读

## web 页面布局基础

当人们谈论网页设计时，他们首先想到布局。布局就是组织网页上的各个元素。首先，当开始设计时你需要掌握一些基本原则。你一旦了解它们，你就能够突破如何设置网页元素这个问题。这篇文章将带你通过几个步骤来学好 web 布局设计。

### 空间和空白符

利用所有的网页空间。换句话说，在你的网页上使用相对大小的网页布局分区，使它们能够放大或缩小以适合浏览器窗口的大小。

注意屏幕分辨率。现在，大多数计算机用户已经不再使用 800×600 分辨率，当你设计的时候要牢记这一点。

### 使用颜色来定义空间

如果你想制作一个有特定宽度的页面，为什么不围绕浏览器屏幕，把页面的背景颜色设置为不同的颜色？这将有助于调整页面大小，以适应不同的浏览器。

### 图像和图形

对齐你的图像。新手最常犯的布局错误就是往网页上塞图片而不管是否可行，没有考虑网页布局。使用对齐属性将有助于使你的图像融为布局的一部分。

### 平衡图像和文字

人们很容易忘乎所以地使用很多图像和动画，但这些图像和动画将使网页难以阅读。当你在考虑你的页面布局时，请记住图像只是你设计重点中的一部分。

### 文本宽度

当你在设计布局时，要确保主要的文本区域显示在一个可读的宽度内。

对大多数人来说，一行 7~11 个字是可以舒适阅读的。长于这个数值，则文本难以阅读，比它短，容易导致脱节和注意力分散。

将文字排版为环绕式是不可取的。这很难做好，而且常常难以阅读。

相关链接

## Adobe

（来源：http://www.adobe.com）

Adobe 系统公司成立于 1982 年。作为软件服务的领导者，25 年来，公司的软件和技术为人们的沟通和合作设立了新的标准，进而给不同媒体部门的人以及人们的生活、工作和娱乐带来重要而有趣的体验。

Adobe 软件的影响力无处不在。无论你是在协同工作，还是在线交易，又或者是和朋友交谈，Adobe 的软件与技术将数字交流注入更丰富、高品质的跨平台互动沟通中，真正实现了随时随地地自由交互。

凭借其卓越的声誉和旗下一系列广受认可的软件品牌，Adobe 已跻身为全球最大、最多元化的软件公司之一。

Adobe 一直致力于创新,时至今天他们的创新信念仍如同 1982 年 Chuck Geschke 和 John Warnock 创立公司时一样强烈。当时他们试图解决一个创新人士所熟知的问题,即如何优美准确地打印出电脑屏幕上的文字与图像。一年以后,带来桌面出版革命的 Adobe PostScript 诞生了。这项全新的文字与图片打印方案给出版业带来翻天覆地的变化。

这只是一个开始,早些年间,Adobe 视自己为行业的远见者和引领者,致力于解决前人看来不可逾越的问题。Adobe 推出了两个爆炸性的应用程序——Adobe Illustrator 和 Adobe Photoshop,在质量和复杂程度方面永久性地颠覆了人们处理图像的方案。并且后来 Adobe 还为视频、电影、网络和其他数字频道创建内容。设计行业永远都不会停滞不前。

随着计算机的交互沟通性以及人们对于实现在线共享文件、互动交流需求的增强,一个新的问题产生了:如何共享这些内容?系统不兼容、软件不支持、电子邮件和新增网页的泛滥使得情况更加糟糕。Adobe 突破性的软件——便携式文档格式(PDF)技术提供了这一问题的解决方案,使企业能够提供跨操作系统和设备的、与平台无关的文件。这样,企业在文件共享和协作方面获得了新机遇。今天,随着诸如网络会议、安全性文件的传输、进度管理等功能的实现,Adobe 从动态交互方面获得的收益得到了扩大。

随着互联网爆炸式的发展成为富有活力的经济引擎,Adobe 公司很快意识到静态的 HTML 网页不能提供用户互动和商业上需要的系统集成。此时 Adobe 再次发挥了带头作用,先是 Adobe Dreamweaver 和 Flash,然后又是 Flex 和 Flash 媒体播放器,让企业的成本控制和网站的可靠发展成为了现实。

Adobe 公司的客户来自各行各业,包括一些全球知名品牌如联邦快递、索尼电影、德国电信、易贝和纽约时报。如今,Adobe 一半以上的收入来自美国境外。Adobe 将利用自己的工具和技术向客户提供丰富的内容和服务。

练习一
1. E   2. E   3. D   4. D   5. D   6. E   7. ③-④-⑤-②-⑥-①-⑨-⑩-⑦-⑧

练习二
1. ×   2. ×   3. √   4. ×   5. √

练习三
1. Images are only one part of web design, you should not put many images on your web page. Most web pages have large amounts of text, you should not put all words in a web page.

2. Full use of the space of a web page. Set screen resolution reasonably. Distinguish the background color and the page color. Balance the graphics and the text. Put the text in a readable width. Avoid centering text in a web page.

练习四
1. C   2. ABCD   3. C   4. D   5. D

# Unit Five
## Managing Online Business

Blog: Open an E-shop

Intensive Reading: Running a Business on the Internet

Extensive Reading: Trends in Social Media Use in China

Related Links: Popular Social Media Platforms

## Open an E-shop

A report from **McKinsey** tells, China's e-tailing market has the world's highest growth rate. There is a tremendous opportunity for individuals and companies to expand their e-Commerce operations in China. Look back my college, internet has gradually played its increasing role in my daily life.

I have been shopping online for several months, and found it very **interesting**. Last week, my shoes were **stained** from the **laundry** and I felt very sad. My roommate Jessie **recommended** me an **E-shop** to get a new pair of shoes. It had **well-known** brands but was only half the price compared to retail **outlets**! The shoes arrived yesterday in **perfect** shape and the **quality** is as good as the ones bought in the stores.

**Recently**, my classmates started talking about opening an E-shop. It has already become a **trend** all over China. People from **every sector** have shown their interests and **energy** on this. One **popular** saying is people going to work in the day while doing business online in the night. Some of them have **successfully** started their own business and some could earn extra **income** each month. **Meanwhile**, a **wave** of opening an E-shop has **swept over** colleges.

Lin, a **senior student** from the third year in our college has already opened an E-shop selling shoes. His shop offered branded leather shoes and **accessories** such as socks and shoe **polish**.

[1] **McKinsey**：麦肯锡，世界著名管理咨询顾问公司

[2] **interesting**：['intristiŋ] adj. 有趣的
[3] **stained**：stain [stein] 的过去分词形式，v. 被染色的
[4] **laundry**：['lɔ:ndri] n. 洗衣房
[5] **recommended**：recommend [rekə'mend] 的过去式，v. 推荐
[6] **E-shop**：网店
[7] **well-known**：[,wel'nəun] adj. 众所周知的
[8] **outlets**：outlet ['autlet] 的复数，n. 经销店，专营店
[9] **perfect**：['pə:fikt] adj. 完美的，理想的，正确的
[10] **quality**：['kwɔliti] n. 品质，特质
[11] **Recently**：['ri:səntli] adv. 最近
[12] **trend**：[trend] n. 趋势
[13] **every sector**：各行各业
[14] **energy**：['enədʒi] n. 活力，精力，能力，能量
[15] **popular**：['pɔpjulə] adj. 大众的，流行的
[16] **successfully**：[sək'sesfuli] adv. 成功地
[17] **income**：['inkəm] n. 收入，所得
[18] **Meanwhile**：['mi:nwail] adv. 同时
[19] **wave**：[weiv] n. 潮流
[20] **swept over**：向……扩展（扫过）
[21] **senior student**：学长
[22] **accessories**：accessory [æk'sesəri] 的复数，n. 配件，零件
[23] **polish**：['pɔliʃ] n. 鞋油

[1] **interview**：['ɪntəvjuː] *n.* 面谈，访问

[2] **summarized**：summarize ['sʌməraɪz] 的过去分词形式，*v.* 概述，摘要而言

[3] **supply**：[sə'plaɪ] *n.* 补给，供给，供应，储备

[4] **Registering**：register ['redʒɪstə] 的 ing 形式，*v.* 登记，注册

[5] **Decorating**：decorate ['dekəreɪt] 的 ing 形式，*v.* 装修

[6] **designing**：design [dɪ'zaɪn] 的 ing 形式，*v.* 设计，计划

[7] **interface**：['ɪntəfeɪs] *n.* 界面

[8] **promotion**：[prə'məʊʃən] *n.* 推广活动

[9] **intrigued**：[ɪn'triːgd] *adj.* 好奇的

[10] **frustrating**：[frʌs'treɪtɪŋ] *adj.* 使人沮丧的，令人泄气的

[11] **search engines**：搜索引擎

[12] **sales figure**：销售数字

[13] **product line**：产品种类

[14] **confident**：['kɒnfɪdənt] *adj.* 确信的，自信的

I had an **interview** with Lin regarding issues to consider in opening an E-shop. It seemed to be fairly basic and it's **summarized** as:

- Finding the **supply**.
- **Registering** an E-shop.
- **Decorating** and **designing** the **interface**.
- Offering **promotion** and sales.

I was **intrigued** and thought about opening my online shop. When I told my parents my decision, they showed their support although they knew little about online business. It was **frustrating** to decide which product to sell. I did extensive research over **search engines**, and looked at **sales figure** on different **product line**. I also asked for advice from Lin and my classmates. It came out with clothes as my first choice. I had no difficulty finding the supplies as my aunt owns a clothes shop. I called my aunt and she was happy with my suggestion. With her support, I was more **confident** in setting up the business.

The next step is to choose a proper **trade platform**. For personal seller, there are several options to start online business. One option is creating a personal website which requires high density of promotion and **capital**, or you can find a **third-party trade platform** where an E-shop model is provided. The main differences are on the **ownership** and **governing** of the business. As a sophomore student, I have limited experience in business as I only worked **part-time jobs** and don't know much about computer technology. Thus, I chose a popular third-party trade platform to get my business started.

I have much experience doing online shopping, thus, it's easy for me to register with the online sales platform. To become a seller, it's different from just buying. You have to provide your personal **identification** and **comply with** a certain requirement in the process of **application**. E-shop is like a **bricks-and-mortar** shop although **diversity** occurs. Decoration is the key to attract customers. Most trade platforms offer free and paid sets of **decoration models** as options. I've seen many great examples on how decoration can be done on popular E-shops. I chose the free model as I have confidence on my product and service.

To be a seller, you have to present product photographs and detailed **descriptions**. I took the photographs and made **modifications** using **Photoshop**. It took me

[1] trade platform：交易平台

[2] capital：['kæpitəl] n. 资本
[3] third-party trade platform：第三方交易平台

[4] ownership：['əunəʃip] n. 所有权
[5] governing：['gʌvəniŋ] n. 治理，管理

[6] part-time jobs：兼职

[7] identification：[ai,dentifi'keiʃən] n. 身份证明
[8] comply with：服从，遵从
[9] application：[,æpli'keiʃən] n. 应用，申请
[10] bricks-and-mortar：实体的，具体的
[11] diversity：[dai'və:siti] n. 差异，多样性
[12] decoration models：装修模板

[13] descriptions：description [dis'kripʃən] 的复数，n. 描写，描述，说明书
[14] modifications：modification [,mɔdifi'keiʃən] 的复数，n. 修正，修饰，修改
[15] Photoshop：图像处理软件

[1] upload: [ˈʌpˌləud] v. 上传

[2] Instant Messengers: 即时通信软件

[3] delivery: [diˈlivəri] n. 递送，交付
[4] payment: [ˈpeimənt] n. 货款
[5] feedback: [ˈfiːdbæk] n. 反馈

several nights to complete all the modification and **upload** all the products online. I was so satisfied once my E-shop started operating. I promoted the E-shop using internet tools, such as E-mail, **Instant Messengers**, blog to inform my friends and classmates. I finally sold one skirt on the third week after the opening. I was so happy and even offered the customer a free **delivery**. When I got my first **payment** and customer **feedback**, I told everybody to share my joy.

People say that opening an E-shop is much easier than bricks-and-mortar store. I have found it's not that easy to be a seller, but I have more confidence now. I believe I will earn a lot from this experience, not just money, but more.

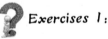 Exercises 1:

Speaking: Give a conversation on web shopping, work in partner and play in role (50~80 words).
Writing: Write down your first web shopping experience with your own words (50~80 words).

## Notes

(1) interesting 令人感兴趣的,有趣的,有吸引力的。Interest 兴趣,Interested 感兴趣的。

(2) laundry 洗衣店,待洗的衣服。washing machine 洗衣机。

(3) recommend 推荐,介绍,建议。recommendation 推荐。

(4) well-known familiar or famous 出名的,众所周知的。

(5) outlet 经销店,专营店,如 retail outlet。也有名牌折扣店的意思,如 Fapai Outlets 法派品牌折扣店。

(6) trend 趋势,动向。latest trend 最新趋势。set a/the trend 开风气之先,显示某种趋势。

(7) successfully 成功的,胜利的。名词为 success,形容词为 successful,动词 succeed 还有继承的意思。

(8) income 收入。Income tax 所得税。与收入相关的词比较多,如 Revenue 收入,多指营业收入;salary 按期支付的收入;Fee 付给律师、医生等的报酬;wages 按小时、日、星期等一定工作量计算的收入,多用于 part-time job 工资的计算;pay-day 领工资的日子。

(9) sweep over 风靡,将……一扫而光。sweep 打扫。sweep the board 囊括奖项。sweeper 清洁工人。也可做名词打扫,如 a clean sweep。

(10) senior student 学长。senior 泛指级别较高的,junior 泛指级别较低的。对于三年制的专科,大三学生可以称为 senior student,在四年制本科大三学生是作为 junior student。

(11) accessory 通常作复数 accessories,配件。也指妇女的服装配搭物(如皮带、手提包等),饰品类产品可统称为 accessories。

(12) summarize 总结、概括,名词形式是 summary。in summary 习语,总的来说。

(13) supply 供应,补给。supply and demand 供求关系。也作动词,supply sth. (to sb.), supply sb. (with sth.)提供。supplier 作"供应商"解。

(14) register 注册,登记。注册一个账户,register an account。registered letter 挂号信。学生开学注册一般用 registration。

(15) interface 界面、分界线,可指网站的显示界面。

(16) promotion 广告宣传,推销活动,提升。网络广告、特价销售等都可以用 promotion 来表示企业所作的宣传活动。

(17) intrigue 激起某人的兴趣或好奇心,也作名词"阴谋"。Intriguing 迷人的。

(18) search engine  搜索引擎，知名的有 Google、Baidu、Bing 等。

(19) sales figure  销售数据，指一定期间的企业营业额。

(20) product line  产品种类，即企业所生产销售的产品或产品组合。

(21) third-party trade platform  第三方交易平台，买卖双方之外的第三方，网站本身只提供交易平台，如淘宝网、易趣网、环球资源等。

(22) identification  身份证明，缩写为 ID。身份证、护照都是 identification。在网上进行注册时，也需要提供相应的身份信息。

(23) application  申请，应用。application form 申请表格。动词形式为 apply。

(24) bricks-and-mortar  实体店铺，与 cricks-and-bricks 相对应，是电子商务理论中特有的模式。后者如新华书店的网上销售与线下销售结合的模式。还有一种 pure cricks 的模式，指 Amazon.com 这样纯粹网络经营的运营模式。

(25) decoration model  装修模板。这里特指在网店装修中，为了装饰网上店铺而提供的装修模板，通过付费或免费方式获得，可以由第三方平台提供，网上也有专门出售装修模板，也可自行设计。

(26) description  描述，说明，形容。detailed description 详细说明。这里指对产品的详细描述。动词形式为 describe。

(27) modification  修饰，修改。extensive modification 大改动。minor modification 些许改动。动词形式为 modify。

(28) Photoshop  目前使用率比较高的一款图像处理软件，为 Adobe 公司旗下软件，集图像扫描、编辑修改、图像制作、广告创意、图像输入与输出于一体的图形图像处理软件。同类软件有 CorelDRAW、Adobe Illustrator、ACDSee、AutoCAD。

(29) upload  上传。特指通过信息技术进行图片、软件等资源的传输，将个人计算机中的信息传递到远程计算机上，使得网络上的人都能够看到。与 download 对应，意为下载。

(30) instant messenger  即时通信软件。即通过对即时通信应用软件的应用来实现网络上的即时沟通，此类软件有 QQ、ICQ、MSN、Google talk、Yahoo、Messenger 等。instant messaging 为动词形式，开展即时通信。

(31) delivery  配送，交付(信件、货物等)。express delivery 快递。cash on delivery 货到付款。delivery terms 配送条款。delivery note 送货单，快递单。

(32) payment  货款，支付。payment by installments 分期付款。

(33) feedback  反馈。一般指顾客在使用产品、服务过后对供应商、卖家的反馈。如 customer feedback 客户反馈，在网店经营中，信用评价中的客户评价可以作为一种反馈。

## Tips for Translation

(1) 用 have been 的句型来表示现在完成时。have been done 为现在完成时的被动形式，表示已经被完成；而 have been doing 现在完成进行时，表示到现在为止仍然在进行。"I have been shopping online for several months." 表示到现在为止，我经常性地进行网络购物。

(2) bricks-and-mortar 直译是砖块加灰泥，但它的意思是指传统经营模式的实体店(不通过英特网的)，属于专有名词。

(3) 按照上下文语境来做翻译。如 delivery 是配送的意思，那么文中 free delivery 可作免费配送，或者免邮来理解。

(4) 对于网络平台这个词的解释可以用 platform，贸易平台可以翻译为 trade/sales platform，第三方平台可以翻译为 third-party platform，第三方在线支付平台则翻译为 third-party online payment platform，而网站是直接翻译为 website 或者 site。

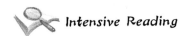

## Intensive Reading

### *Running a Business on the Internet*

There is no **doubt** that Internet business is **thriving**. E-business has lower costs than **traditional** stores as **rental expense**, **manpower salary** and **operating costs** are lower.

Your online business can be very successful, if you can find a unique selling point. First, you have to be sure what product to sell online. Your product line is the **engine** of your business. Thus, you have to make sure what to sell first. **Pay attention to** the following aspects and you may find it easier:

**Competitive price**: The **advantage** of E-business enables sellers to offer much lower price than traditional store. For the same product, the price is lower hence increasing its **competitiveness**.

**Special or trendy products**: web **consumers** would like to find unique or trendy products online.

**Virtual/digital products**: virtual products such as software, CD, ebook, etc. sold through network without **shipping expense** is suitable for online business.

[1] **doubt**：[daut] *n.* 怀疑，疑问
[2] **thriving**：['θraiviŋ] *adj.* 欣欣向荣的
[3] **traditional**：[trə'diʃən(ə)l] *adj.* 传统的
[4] **rental expense**：租金
[5] **manpower salary**：人工工资
[6] **operating costs**：运营成本
[7] **engine**：['endʒin] *n.* 核心
[8] **Pay attention to**：注意，关心
[9] **Competitive price**：有竞争力的价格
[10] **advantage**：[əd'vɑːntidʒ] *n.* 优势
[11] **competitiveness**：竞争力
[12] **Special or trendy products**：特殊或者流行产品
[13] **consumers**：消费者
[14] **Virtual/digital products**：虚拟/数字产品
[15] **shipping expense**：运费

**Small items**: more **convenient** for delivery and lower shipping fees.

**Higher value-added**: the value of the product should not be lower than shipping fees.

To **sum up**, items suitable for online sales includes books, CDs, music, software, **3C digital products**, **Hi-tech products**, clothes, beauty products, jewelry, etc..

As long as you have decided your product line, you can start to promote the products and brand. Online marketing is the most **cost-effective** way among advertising media with **SEO (Search Engine Optimization)** and **PPC (Pay Per Click)** as the main advertising force. Meanwhile, good service is very important to web consumers.

[1] **Small items**：小件商品
[2] **convenient**：方便
[3] **Higher value-added**：附加值较高的产品
[4] **sum up**：总结
[5] **3C digital products**：3C 数码产品
[6] **Hi-tech products**：高科技产品

[7] **cost-effective**：成本效益好的
[8] **SEO (Search Engine Optimization)**：搜索引擎优化
[9] **PPC (Pay Per Click)**：点击支付

Apart from above factors, to be successful online, your business also needs capital investment, **information system**, **supply chain management** and **administration supports**.

Finally, you have to be good at and **passionate** at what you are doing.

[10] **information system**：信息系统
[11] **supply chain management**：供应链管理
[12] **administration supports**：行政支持
[13] **passionate**：['pæʃənit] *adj.* 充满激情的

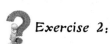 Exercise 2：

List at least 10 products suitable for sales online.

## Notes

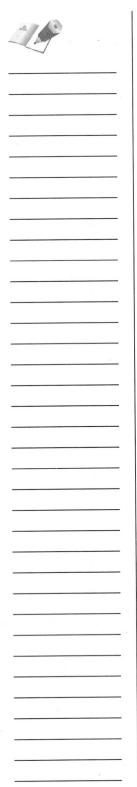

(1) traditional 传统的。在电子商务中，通常用 E-business 与 traditional business 形成对应，作为新兴电子商务与传统商务的对比。

(2) rental expense, manpower salary and operating costs 企业经营成本中的租金支出、人力成本支出、运营成本支出。企业的经营成本还可以包括财务成本等。

(3) engine 这个词通常作发动机、引擎来解释，在这里理解为核心。

(4) competitive 有竞争力的。这个词经常用在商业模型中，competitive advantage 意指竞争优势。名词形式为 competitiveness，理解为竞争力。

(5) virtual/digital product 虚拟/数字产品。这一类产品可以直接通过网络进行产品的转移，是非常适合电子商务行业的一类产品。

(6) value-added 附加值。即通过企业的内部生产活动等创造的产品附加值和通过市场战略在流通领域创造的商品附加值。适合电子商务销售的产品，它的附加值只有高于物流成本，才能有销售利润。

(7) 3C digital products 3C 类数码产品。3C 指的是计算机 (Computer)、通信 (Communication) 和消费类电子产品 (Consumer Electronics) 三者结合，也称"信息家电"。代表性网站是绿森商城 (www.green3c.com)。

(8) hi-tech products 高科技产品，如电子商务软件系统、数码相框等。

(9) SEO: Search Engine Optimization 搜索引擎优化。这是网络营销的一种手段，是一种利用搜索引擎的搜索规则来提高目的网站在有关搜索引擎内的排名的方式。

(10) PPC: Pay Per Click 中文意思就是点击付费广告。点击付费广告是大公司最常用的网络广告形式。提供点击付费的网站非常多，主要有各大门户网站(如搜狐、新浪)、搜索引擎(谷歌和百度)以及其他浏览量较大的网站。

(11) supply chain management 供应链管理。供应链管理就是指对整个供应链系统进行计划、协调、操作、控制和优化的各种活动和过程，其目标是要将顾客所需的正确的产品(Right Product)，能够在正确的时间(Right Time)、按照正确的数量(Right Quantity)、正确的质量(Right Quality)和正确的状态(Right Status)送到正确的地点(Right Place)，并使总成本达到最佳化。

(12) administration 行政管理，也作管理部门解释。administration office 行政办公室。administrator 行政管理人员。

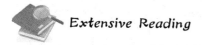

Extensive Reading

## Trends in Social Media Use in China

(Source: Social media and web marketing in China, Hanover Research, October 2013)

The **social media platforms** that appear to be most promising for reaching out to Chinese applicants include **Sina Weibo**(similar to Twitter), **Renren**(similar to Facebook),and **Youku**(similar to YouTube).

[1] **social media platforms**：社交媒体平台

[2] **Sina Weibo**：新浪微博
[3] **Renren**：人人网
[4] **Youku**：优酷网

Social media use in China is constantly rising——at last count, there were nearly 600 million active users, a figure that is up 60 percent just from 2012. A 2012 survey by McKinsey and Company that investigated various characteristics of social networking behavior revealed that an estimated 91 percent of the total population visited a social media platform in the previous six months, and 95 percent of internet users in China who live in the nation's largest cities have a social media account. Most of China's internet users access the internet through a personal computer, though a personal computer, though **mobile devices** are also gaining popularity: according to McKinsey, about 50 percent of mobile-phone users in the survey said they were planning to buy a **smartphone** in the next six months, 35 percent said they have used a **tablet computer**, and one-fourth of consumers who do not own a tablet computer said they plan to buy one in the next year.

Chinese social media users also tend to be very active: the McKinsey survey reported that users in China generally spend approximately 46 minutes per day on social media sites, compared to 37 minutes in the United States and just seven minutes in Japan.

Overall, the social media market in China has been described as "very **fragmented** and local". According to a McKinsey and Company brief, "each social-media and e-commerce platform has at least two major local players: in **microblogging**(or weibo),for example, Sina Weibo and Tencent Weibo; in social networking, a number of companies, including Renren and **Kaixin001**. These players have different strengths, areas of focus, and, often, geographic priorities." A brief overview of the top sites is provided in the figure below.

---

[1] **mobile devices**：移动设备

[2] **smartphone**：智能手机
[3] **tablet computer**：掌上电脑

[4] **fragmented**：碎片的

[5] **microblogging**：微博

[6] **Kaixin001**：开心网

## Overview of Top Chinese Social Media Sites

| PLATFORM | DESCRIPTION |
|---|---|
| Douban | Open forum for movie, music, and book |
| Jiayuan | The largest internet dating website of China |
| Kaixin001 | Cloned the most successful and well-known Facebook applications to the Chinese market |
| Pengyou | A real-name social network |
| Qzone | Social networking website where users can write blogs and share photos, music, etc. |
| Renren | Facebook of China |
| Sina Weibo | Chinese microblogging website(similar to Twitter), with ability to included images and video |
| Tencent Weibo | Chinese microblogging website (similar to Twitter) |
| WeChat | Mobile voice and text app with social networking features, including photo-sharing |

Source: Go-Globe.com and Mashable

Over 80 percent of Chinese social media users are active on more than one site, and **local** platforms dominate the market. Though specific numbers vary (in part because of issues with virtual, or fake, followers), it is clear that **Qzone**, a social blogging site, and microblogging platforms Tencent Weibo and Sina Weibo are favorites among users. For instance, the McKinsey survey revealed that 44 percent of respondents use Qzone the most, followed by Sina Weibo and Renren(19 percent each), Tencent Weibo (8 percent), and Kaixin(7 percent).

[1] **local**：本土的

[2] **Qzone**：QQ 空间

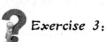 *Exercise 3*:

List the social networking sites you know and introduce it.

 Related Links

## Popular Social Media Platforms

(Source: Social media and web marketing in China, Hanover Research, October 2013)

In the following paragraphs, we introduce some of the top platforms for reaching out to Chinese high school students.

### BAIDU

Baidu is China's equivalent of Google, and also offers other services includes "**Baidu Tieba**" ("Post Bar", a discussion forum) and "**Baidu Zhidao**" ( "Baidu Knows", a question and answer site).

### RENREN

Renren and Qzone are both considered the Chinese versions of Facebook. Chinese teenagers typically begin using social media with Qzone and QQ (China's top **instant messaging** program), two platforms that boast high concentrations of users below the age of 18. As they get older, college students **outgrow** Qzone and move on to Renren, which is dominated by the young adult population.

Tencent's Qzone may boast a larger count of Registered users, but the site has been criticized as being heavily populated by "dormant, skeleton profiles" with "low value and retention rates". The site, which is acessed primarily by teenage, rural, and casual users, allows the use of **nicknames** and aliases rather than real

[1] **BAIDU**：百度

[2] **Baidu Tieba**：百度贴吧

[3] **Baidu Zhidao**：百度知道

[4] **instant messaging**：即时通信

[5] **outgrow**：长大逐渐不再需要

[6] **nicknames**：昵称

**identities**. Meanwhile, Renren is more popular among college students, "as it serves as an ideal resource for accessing news about their respective universities, including curriculum updates, supplementary materials and class discussion boards". College students often retain their Qzone and QQ accounts-usually, they will log in to QQ to stay in touch with their old friends, parents and classmates, but neglect their Qzone pages and use Renren instead. Renren users tend to be more "transparent and honest" when using Renren, while they are more likely to filter their messages on Qzone.

WEIBO

Weibo, which means "microblog" is the Chinese version of Twitter and is offered under several platforms. The two biggest players are Sina Weibo and Tencent Weibo. Like Twitter, Weibo allows users to post 140-character microblogs, pictures, and videos. One of the differences in user activity, however, is that while Twitter users often post about news, Sina Weibo users tend to comment more on entertainment topics. Similarly, some of the users with the most "**followers**".

On Tencent Weibo are **celebrities**, hosts, famous companies, and media and entertainment agencies.

Sina Weibo is particularly common among university students, young professionals, and urban dwellers, while Tencent users tend to be more rural.

[1] **identities**：身份

[2] **followers**：粉丝
[3] **celebrities**：明星

It is estimated that 70 to 80 percent of China's university students have a Weibo account, and between 40 and 50 percent of students use it every day.

YOUKU

Youku is China's equivalent of YouTube, though there are some distinct differences. First, while YouTube's videos are primarily user-generated, 70 percent of Youku's content is syndicated (i.e., professionally produced). Youku also primarily features "longer" videos, rather than short clips or music videos.

### Exercise 4:

Choose the best option and fill in the bracket with the mark No..

1. The business model of Taobao.com is (　　).

A. B2B　　　　B. B2C　　　　C. C2C　　　　D. B2B2C

2. eBay.com is a typical E-business model of (　　).

A. pure clicks　　　B. clicks and bricks　　　C. bricks and mortar

3. Which option is different from others? (　　)

A. Alibaba.com　　　　　　　　B. jd.com

C. hc360.com　　　　　　　　　D. Globalresources.com

4. Products suitable for online selling should not be (　　).

A. Higher value-added　　　　　B. Jewelry

C. Low price　　　　　　　　　D. Poor quality

5. What third-party trade platform can help sellers do? (　　)

A. Delivery　　　　　　　　　　B. Directly sell to buyers

C. Build up website　　　　　　D. Find buyers globally

# 参考译文及答案

# 单元五　网店运营

博客

## 网上开店

　　网上购物几个月了，我觉得很有趣。上个星期，我的鞋子洗变色了，正觉得很难过的时候，室友 Jessie 向我推荐了一家卖鞋的网上商店。这家店铺销售名牌鞋，价格却是实体专卖店的一半。昨天，我收到了鞋子，外形和质量都跟专卖店的一样。

　　最近，同学们都在讨论开网店的事。这在中国已经成为流行了。来自各行各业的人们都显示出了他们的兴趣和热情。据说很多人白天上班，晚上开店，其中一些已经成功将开网店变成自己的事业，而另外一些每个月也都可以得到一定的额外收入。同时，这股风潮也席卷了大学校园。

　　我们学院大三的林学长也开了一家网店，主要卖品牌皮鞋和配件，如袜子、鞋油等。

　　针对如何开设网店我采访过林学长。他给出的几点要素似乎都很基本。

- 寻找货源。
- 注册一家网店。
- 装修、设计店铺。
- 进行网上推广和销售。

　　受到大家的影响，我也很想开一家网店。当我告诉父母这项决定时，他们虽然不太了解电子商务，但是很支持我。找产品是一件很有挫败感的事情。我通过搜索引擎查询很多的资料，看了相关的销售数据和产品，还咨询了林学长和其他同学，最后，服装成为我的首选。因为我的阿姨经营着一家服装店，经过联系，她很支持我，货源就有了。有了这一步，我的信心大增。

　　下一步是选择合适的交易平台。对个人来说，网络创业有很多方法。一种是自建网站，需要在网络推广和资金上有较大的投入；也可以在第三方平台上直接开网店。两种方式的主要区别在于店铺的所有权和监管措施。作为高职院校的学生，我的工作经验很少，只做过兼职工作，对计算机技术也不太在行。因此，我选择第三方平台来开立我的网上店铺。

　　有了之前的购物经验，网上平台的注册对我来说很简单了。但是，作为卖家，跟单纯买东西不同，在注册过程中，需要根据平台的要求提供身份证明等信息。网上商店跟实体店很像的是，装修对于吸引顾客来说很重要。大多数交易平台都有免费和收费的装修模板可选。我知道很多知名的网店，它们的装修就很吸引人。我对我的产品和服务很有信心，于是，我选择了免费模板。

　　作为卖家，上传产品照片和产品详细描述是一定要做的。我拍摄了照片，并花了好几个晚上用 Photoshop 软件进行了编辑、修改和上传。很高兴我的店铺终于开张了，于是，我通过邮件、即时通信软件、博客等网络工具，把这个好消息告诉了我的朋友们和同学们。开张后的第三个星期，我终于卖出了一条裙子。我太高兴了，就给买家免了运费。当我收到第一笔款项和客户评价时，我几乎告诉每一个我知道的人，让大家分享我的快乐。

很多人说，开网店比开实体店简单多了，我却认为开网店并不简单。但是我更有信心了，我相信我会得到很多，不仅仅是钱。

*精读*

### 在互联网上做生意

互联网经济的兴盛是毋庸置疑的。电子商务与传统商务相比，在租金支出、人力支出和运营成本等方面大大地降低了。

想要让你的网上生意获得成功，找到一个好的卖点很重要。首先应该确定卖什么产品，因为产品是企业经营的核心。以下几类产品可以考虑。

具备价格竞争力的产品：电子商务的优势就是让卖家提供比实体店更便宜的商品。同样的产品，价格越低，越有竞争力。

特殊或者流行产品：网络消费者期望在网上找到独特的或者流行的产品。

虚拟/数字产品：虚拟产品像软件、CD、电子书等可以直接通过网络实现物流配送。

小件商品：方便配送，且运送成本较低。

附加值较高产品：产品的价值不能低于运费。

总之，适合网上销售的产品包括书籍、CD、音乐、软件、3C 数码产品、高科技产品、服装、化妆品、珠宝等。

当你确定了产品种类后，就可以开始推广产品和品牌了。网络营销是最省成本的广告媒体，其中以搜索引擎优化和点击付费广告为最主要的方式。同时，对网络消费者来说，服务也很重要。

除了以上因素，企业想要成功，还需要进行资金投入、信息系统建设、供应链管理和行政支持等。

最后，你一定要擅长你的工作并且对你所做的事情充满热情。

*泛读*

### 中国社交媒体的发展趋势

目前中国最具潜质的社交媒体平台包括新浪微博(类似 Twitter)，人人(类似 Facebook)，和优酷(类似 YouTube)。

在中国，社交媒体的使用率不断增加——最近一次统计显示有 6 亿在线活跃用户，相较 2012 年增加了 60%。麦肯锡 2012 年针对社交网络行为的调查显示，约 91%的人在最近 6 个月内登录过社交媒体网站，95%的大城市网络用户拥有社交网络账号。根据麦肯锡报告，大部分中国用户通过个人电脑登录网站，而手机端的流量也在持续增长。调研显示 50%的手机用户表示计划在接下来的 6 个月内购买智能手机，35%的用户表示他们拥有掌上电脑，四分之一的消费者表示他们准备在明年购买掌上电脑。

中国社交媒体用户的表现十分活跃：麦肯锡报告显示，中国用户每天花费 46 分钟在社交媒体上，超过美国的 37 分钟和日本的 7 分钟。

总体上，中国的社交网络市场被描述成"碎片化和本土化"，根据麦肯锡公司的简报："每一个社交媒体和电商平台都至少有两大本土业者，例如微博有新浪和腾讯，社交网络有人人网和开心网等数家。他们都有各自的优势领域，往往是在地理区域方面。"下表针对中国主要社交媒体进行举例。

中国主要社交媒体网站回顾

| 平台 | 描述 |
|---|---|
| 豆瓣 | 电影、音乐和读书论坛 |
| 世纪佳缘 | 中国最大的婚恋交友网站 |
| 开心网 | 知名社交网站 Facebook 的复制版 |
| 朋友网 | 一个实名社交网络 |
| QQ 空间 | 为用户提供博客空间，分享图片，音乐等内容的社交网站 |
| 人人网 | 中国版 Facebook |
| 新浪微博 | 中国微博客网站（类似 Twitter），可以发图片和视频 |
| 腾讯微博 | 中国微博客网站（类似 Twitter） |
| 微信 | 社交性质的手机语音和短信应用，如图片分享 |

中国 80%的社交媒体用户使用一个以上的社交网站，本土平台在市场上占主导地位。尽管具体数值各地不同（部分原因包括网络的虚拟性，不真实性，从众性），社交博客网站 Qzone 和微博平台腾讯微博及新浪微博是最受欢迎的。例如，麦肯锡调查显示 44%的被调查者使用 Qzone，接下来是新浪微博和人人（19%），腾讯微博（8%）和开心网（7%）。

相关链接

### 最受欢迎的社交平台

下面本文介绍中国高校学生中使用最多的几个社交平台。

百度

百度在中国相当于谷歌，也提供其他服务像百度贴吧（贴吧，就是论坛）和百度知道（知道，问答网站）。

人人网和 QQ 空间都被视为中国版的 Facebook。而中国的青少年用得最多的是 QQ 空间和 QQ（中国最大的即时通信工具），两个平台都聚集了大量 18 岁以下青少年的关注。随着他们的年龄增长，大学生渐渐不再需要 QQ 空间，转向在年轻人中比较受欢迎的人人网。

腾讯空间引以为傲的是它拥有大量注册用户，但是被批评有大量的休眠账户，使用率非常低。网站的主要用户是青少年、农村用户和普通用户，允许用户使用昵称和化名而不是真实姓名。同时，人人网在大学生中更受欢迎。"它可以更方便地获得各个大学的新闻,包括课程更新，材料补充和课堂讨论。"大学生还是会保留 QQ 空间和 QQ 账户——通常，他们还是会登录 QQ 来跟朋友、父母和同学保持联络，但是会使用人人网而不是 QQ 空间。人人网的用户在网站上会更透明和诚实，而 QQ 空间用户会对信息进行过滤。

微博

微博，也就是微博客，是中国版的 Twitter，在中国有多个平台提供此服务。其中最大的两个就是新浪微博和腾讯微博。推特用户可以发布 140 字的微博客，也可以发图片和视频。跟 Twitter 不同的是，Twitter 用户更多的是发新闻，新浪微博用户更关注娱乐话题。相似的是，腾讯微博拥有最多粉丝的账号是明星、机构、知名企业、媒体和娱乐机构。

新浪微博在大学生、青年专家学者以及城市居民中流行，而腾讯微博用户会更草根一些。

据估计，70%～80%的中国大学生拥有微博账号，40%～50%的学生会每天使用。

优酷

优酷相当于 YouTube，但是有自己的特色。首先 YouTube 的视频内容主要是用户原创，而 70%的优酷内容是聚合内容（即专业制作的）。优酷的视频比一般的段视频和音乐视频要更长一点。

练习一　（略）
练习二　（略）
练习三　（略）
练习四　1. C　2. A　3. B　4. D　5. D

# Unit Six
## E-marketing

Blog: My E-marketing

Intensive Reading: The Year 1997 and E-marketing

Extensive Reading: Start Advertising with Search Engine

Related Links: Selling on Amazon.com

## My E-marketing

Today is the first day of my meaningful summer holiday, the **part-time job** of mine will begin. I feel rather excitedly. Because firstly, this first part-time job is the **achievement** of my repeated interviews; secondly, this job is the first time for me to carry out the internship **individually**; lastly, this job is the application of my major subject in college, my job is E-marketing, which provides the opportunity to use **theoretical** knowledge of study. At the same time, I also feel nervous, for the performance of mine will be good or not, or whether the work that I do can bring profit to the company. At all events, I will work **diligently** and try my best to finish all tasks.

Its marketing activities in the traditional style, mainly on newspapers, company **booklet**, trade fair and other off-line media, now the company that I serve spreads to the E-marketing which **appeared** along with the developing of the Internet. The basic idea of E-marketing is to provide the **benefit** conditions for the management of company through the Internet, which acts for the company's whole goal and is the part of the whole marketing **strategy**.

But I also **acquire** that the difference of the E-marketing and marketing is that the former is included

[1] **part-time job**：兼职

[2] **achievement**：[əˈtʃiːvmənt] n. 成就

[3] **individually**：[indiˈvidjuəli] adv. 单个地，个别地

[4] **theoretical**：[θiəˈretikəl] adj. 理论上的

[5] **diligently**：[ˈdilidʒəntli] adv. 勤勉地，勤奋地

[6] **booklet**：[ˈbuklit] n. 小册子

[7] **appeared**：appear [əˈpiə] 的过去式，v. 出现，产生

[8] **benefit**：[ˈbenifit] n. 利益

[9] **strategy**：[ˈstrætidʒi] n. 战略
[10] **acquire**：[əˈkwaiə] v. （通过努力、能力、行为表现）获得，得到

in the marketing, the platform for E-marketing is the Internet, but the marketing can go beyond the former scale. And E-marketing, one way of the marketing but not the sole, is not the so-called ecommerce but belong to the ecommerce.

Through E-marketing, I can **establish** company's brand, make the website promotion, sell products and **submit information on-line**, carry out research and promotion, and **consolidate** business relationship with customers, etc..

There are two methods for me to do E-marketing, one is to build the website of company, and the other is not. Such as the Dell Company that has sold its own products on its own website www.dell.com. More sold its products on other **online service providers' websites**, that rather suitable for the self-employed and others have not enough ability or money to build website. They can use the ecommerce site such as the global sources site to do advertisement, in this situation the only thing marketers have to do is to provide the Ads fee and **materials** for products, and the rate of showing about company's information will be raising on the Internet, and realizing the **function** of E-marketing.

There are various tools for E-marketing, my **favorite** ways are such as using my company owned website, **search engines**, like Google and Baidu, both of them are famous search engines in China and even

---

[1] **establish**:[isˈtæbliʃ] v. 建立

[2] **submit information on-line**:在线信息发布

[3] **consolidate**:[kənˈsɔlideit] v. 使加强,使巩固

[4] **online service providers' websites**:在线服务提供商网站

[5] **materials**:material [məˈtiəriəl] 的复数,n. 材料

[6] **function**:[ˈfʌŋkʃən] n. 作用,功能

[7] **favorite**:[ˈfeivərit] adj. 最喜爱的

[8] **search engines**:搜索引擎

in the world. I can also use E-mails to send the marketing information, one way is the inner E-mail list owned to the company, by which I can gather many E-mail addresses as my own resource to **multi-send to E-mail addresses**, but it need much time as it's not easy to accumulate so many addresses in short days. The other way is to use the external mailing lists that belong to E-mail servers which can stand for my company to send marketing information out to mass, so we can save a lot of time and energy to do the other tasks. **Blog marketing** also can be used, the special platform as www.bokee.com or blog menu on the E-commerce site as www.alibaba.com is the better choice for us to do E-marketing job.

In addition, along with the development of **Web 2.0、Web3.0** technology, came out many E-marketing methods. Really Simple Syndication tool is the one, such as POTU RSS reading explorer, and BBS, **instant message** tool QQ, Aliwangwang, Skype, MSN, E-books, Micro-blog, WeChat, text message marketing and DingTalk can be used according to the company special situation. If allowed, I can use **4G mobile phone**, etc., the wireless communication tools, to make advertisements on the **WAP sites**.

[1] **multi-send to E-mail addresses**：群发电子邮件

[2] **Blog marketing**：博客营销

[3] **Web2.0、Web3.0**：Web 2.0 是相对 Web 1.0（2003 年以前的互联网模式）的新的一类互联网应用的统称

[4] **instant message**：即时通信

[5] **4G mobile phone**：4G 移动电话

[6] **WAP sites**：无线应用网站

 Exercises 1:

Speaking: Think about the function of E-marketing during the development of enterprises and express it with your own words in English (50~100 words).

Writing: Write an article about the future of E-marketing (not less than 100 words).

## Notes

(1) part-time 兼职的，部分时间的。full-time 全职的。

(2) achievement 成就，成绩。可数名词。

(3) interviews interview 的复数形式。Interview 面谈，面试。

(4) carry out 执行，实现。carry off 拿走，夺走。

(5) application （尤指理论、发现等的）应用，运用。后常接 of sth./to do sth.。词组 Application Program Interface 应用程序界面。

(6) subject 学科，科目，课程。可能受……影响的，易遭受……的，如… to sth.；使臣服，使顺从，如… sth. (to sth. )。

(7) provide 提供，供应，给予，如… sb. with sth./ … sth. for sb.。

(8) opportunity 机会，时机。常见搭配… to do sth. / … for sth. /for doing sth. / … of doing sth.。equal opportunity 机会均等。

(9) performance 表现，演出，表演。high performance 速度很快的，高性能的。

(10) profit 利润，收益，赢利，获益，得到好处；对……有用(或有益)，如… by/from sth.。

(11) diligently 孜孜不倦地，勤奋地，修饰某人努力勤奋。

(12) activities 名词原型是 activity。活动，活动力，行动。

(13) booklet 小册子，booklet 广告小册子。

(14) trade fair 商品交易会。

(15) appeared 动词 appear 的过去分词。出现，显露，出席。

(16) benefit 有益于，得益，如… from/by sth.。

(17) strategy 策略，… for doing sth. / … to do sth.。

(18) platform 平台。platform interconnectivity software 平台互连软件。

(19) establish 建立，创立，设立。pre-establish 预定，re-establish 重建，恢复。

(20) brand 品牌。brand name 品牌名称。brand-new 全新的。

(21) website promotion 网站推广。website promotion department 网站推广部。

(22) submit information on-line　在线提交信息。

(23) carry out research　开展研究。carry out...research 开展关于……的研究。

(24) consolidate　使加强，使巩固。consolidation 巩固，不可数名词。

(25) www.dell.com　戴尔公司网址。该公司是全球领先的IT产品及服务提供商。

(26) online service provider　在线服务提供商。Internet Service Provider 互联网服务提供者。

(27) global sources site　环球资源，B2B电子商务平台。

(28) advertisement　广告。classified advertisement 分类广告。

(29) situation　情况，状况。save the situation 挽回败局，扭转局面。

(30) Ads fee　广告费。Ads 是 advertisements 的缩写。

(31) function　功能。function key 功能键。multiple-function devices 多功能设备。

(32) inner E-mail list　内部邮件列表。

(33) resource　资源，向……提供资金(或设备)。enterprise resource planning software 企业资源规划软件。

(34) multi-send to E-mail addresses　群发电子邮件。E-mail marketing 电子邮件营销。voice multi-broadcast Fax System 语音传真群发系统。

(35) www.bokee.com　博客网域名。

(36) Really Simple Syndication　简单资源聚合，一种网上资源订阅技术。

(37) instant message　即时通信。

(38) wireless communication tools　无线通信工具，如无线路由等。

(39) WAP sites　无线应用网站。

## Tips for Translation

(1) Its marketing activities in the traditional style…是无动分句。该类句子前部短语省略了主语和谓语，在翻译成汉语时应该把主谓语补上，使之符合汉语表达习惯。使用这一类短语结构时需要注意，短语中被省略的主语必须是主句中的同一主语。

(2) But I also acquire that the difference of the E-marketing and marketing is that the former is included…句中第一个"that"是宾语从句的引导词，第二个"that"是引导表语从句。

(3) And E-marketing, one way of the marketing but not the sole, is not the so-called ecommerce but belong to the ecommerce. "one way of the marketing but not the sole" 是 E-marketing 的同位语。在这种情况下，同位语通常翻译成句子，如把它翻译成"网络营销是营销的一种而不是唯一的方式"。

(4) In addition，此外，通常放在句首。

(5) 英文翻译成中文时通常要根据句子的语境适当添加和减少词语，以便更准确地表达出原文所包含的意义。如 If allowed, I can use 4G mobile phone…中"If allowed"直译的话就是"如果允许"，比较生硬，可以添词翻译成"如果条件允许"。

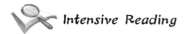 Intensive Reading

## The Year 1997 and E-marketing

For Chinese, the year 1997 is not a normal year, because Hong Kong was returned to the hug of motherland. Also, this year was significant to business field for it was the beginning year of E-marketing.

In February of 1997, China Byte had **sponsored** the free news mailing list to the web users, till to the end of that year, the number of users climbed up to almost 30,000, then in march, the first commercial advertisement, about 468×60**pixel**, was made on this website, which has been called **banner** today. In November, the first free web magazine was provided by "**soyi**", the original special web magazine server. All this symbolized the generation.

Of course, these were the several achievements of **pioneering**, the development of E-marketing is not rising in a direct line, not until to 2000 year, the break of the bubble of Internet, did the vigorous development began. For companies had changed from building websites rush and **aimlessly** which hadn't earn any money to recognizing the web **reasonably**, and pay attention to explore profit from the web, which has stimulated the large scale development of E-marketing servers. Today E-marketing has **played an important role** if companies want to have good status in the commercial field.

[1] **sponsored**: sponsor ['spɔnsəd] 的过去分词形式，v. 举办，发起

[2] **pixel**: ['piksəl] n. 像素
[3] **banner**: ['bænə] n. 旗帜广告
[4] **soyi**: 索易网

[5] **pioneering**: [,paiə'niəriŋ] adj. 开创性的，先驱的

[6] **aimlessly**: ['eimlisli] adv. 漫无目的地
[7] **reasonably**: ['ri:zənəbli] adv. 明辨道理地，有理性地

[8] **played an important role**: 扮演重要角色

 Exercise 2:

Give some examples of classic websites that have provided service of news reserving through the web in English.

## Notes

(1) normal　正常的，如 normal temperature 正常体温。也做名词用，常态，如 as per normal/usual 照常，按惯例，一如既往。

(2) hug　怀抱，拥抱。

(3) motherland, 祖国，由 mother(母亲)和 land(土地)合成。

(4) significant　重要意义的，significant other 有特殊关系的那一位(如配偶、情人)。

(5) China Byte　比特网，IT 专业信息门户。

(6) banner　网幅广告，旗帜广告，横幅广告(网络广告的主要形式，一般使用 GIF 格式的图像文件，可以使用静态图形，也可用多帧图像拼接为动画图像)。banner headline(报纸头版的)通栏大标题。banner Ad(互联网上的)标题广告。

(7) web magazine　网络杂志。magazine 还有"期刊"之意，同义词有 journal 等。

(8) symbolized　象征。同义词有 represent，typify，emblematize。

(9) pioneering　开拓性的，先驱性的，探索性。pioneer　拓荒者，先驱者，开拓者，轻工兵。

(10) vigorous　充满活力的。近义词组/词有 full of vitality/vigorously 朝气蓬勃地。

(11) recognizing　recognize 的动名词形式，认出，识别，认识。后面常接"as"，表示将某人或物看成……。

(12) reasonably　合理地。同义词有 rationally 合理地，理智地。

(13) pay attention to　注意到……，重视，留心。

(14) the large scale　大规模。前面常接介词 on。

(15) played an important role　扮演重要角色。

 **Extensive Reading**

## Start Advertising with Search Engine

(Partly refer to http://cn.yahoo.com)

Search engine is one of the most popular E-marketing tools for business **entities**. For web users often search various types of information with search engines. Therefore, as marketers you shouldn't miss this cherish chance.

[1] **entities**：entity ['entəti] 的复数, *n.* 实体

Then how to apply search engines? Usually two ways are mainly used. The one mode is that we can submit our domain names freely to Baidu, Google, etc. to promote our company website, I should only have to open the free domain name submit window, enter my domain name and authentication code correctly，then click the "submit" button. The other  way is to participate in the **key words bidding** to make the **content related advertisement**. This way is effectively and energy saved, I can take part in the bidding step by step following the suggestion of related servers. Take Yahoo! for example, the following paragraphs are advertising tips abstracted from Yahoo!.

[2] **key words bidding**：关键词竞价
[3] **content related advertisement**：内容定位广告

Start Advertising with Yahoo! search marketing only in 5 Simple Steps:

(1) Target Customers by Geographic Location Display your AD to customers throughout the entire market, or select specific regions or cities.

(2) **Choose Keywords** related to your Business. Enter words or phrases related to the products and services your business provides.

[4] **Choose Keywords**：选择关键词

What does your business provide? You can enter

[1] **prospective customer**：潜在顾客

[2] **describe**：[dis'kraib] *v.* 描述

[3] **Plasma**：['plæzmə] *n.* 等离子体

[4] **maximum bid**：最高出价

[5] **billing information**：账单信息

[6] **activate**：['æktiveit] *v.* 起动，激动

keywords, specify a product or service you would like to promote.

Imagine yourself as a **prospective customer** who is searching for a specific product or service that your business provides. What words would you use to find? What you're looking for? For best results, each keyword should be precise; it should **describe** a product or service your prospective customers will find when they navigate to your site.

The following examples illustrate how the keywords you choose can focus on the exact products and services your prospective customers are looking for. Too general: "Televisions". Better: "**Plasma** flat screen televisions". So I will carefully choose my keywords and fully display my company's orientation of promotion.

Not sure what to enter? Find keywords related to your own site. Then enter up to 50 keywords or keyword phrases, one per line.

(3) Tell Yahoo! how much you'd like to spend, specify your daily spending limit and **maximum bid**.

(4) Create your Ad, write the Ad that will be displayed to prospective customers.

(5) Activate or save your Ad, review your Ad and activate it by entering your **billing information**, or save it until you are ready to **activate**… Here, I think most of you know how to carry out the task of advertising with search engine. So be confident and let's begin to advertise.

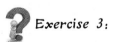 *Exercise 3*:

1. List some websites that can be used as the platform for you to make advertisement on.

## Related Links

### Selling on Amazon.com

(Sources: http://www.amazon.com/)

www.amazon.com is a **world leading** E-commerce site, it was build in the year 1995 by Jeff Bezos the sponsor of amozon.com. Today this site is still the world  famous website for buyers and sellers among the world.

When you sell in the Amazon Marketplace you place your items in front of millions of customers—your items are displayed right **alongside** those carried by Amazon.com! There are no fees unless you sell.

Start selling now:

List your **items**.

(1) Search for the item you want to sell.

When you've found an exact match, click the "Sell yours here" button on the right-hand side of that page. Note: there can be several editions or **formats** of the same item—make sure you have the correct one.

You can also sell your item from Amazon.com's home page by clicking "Sell Your Stuff" on the **navigation bar** or from the Manage Inventory section of your **Seller Account**.

(2) Describe the condition of your item.

Select the condition and enter any **comments regarding** the condition item.

(3) Set your price and register to collect online payment from your buyer **via** marketplace.

Payments by Amazon.

[1] **world leading**：世界领先的

[2] **alongside**：[əˈlɔŋˈsaid] prep. 与……一起，与……同时

[3] **items**：item [ˈaitəm] 的复数，n. 项目

[4] **formats**：format [ˈfɔːmæt] 的复数，n. 格式，样式，版式

[5] **navigation bar**：导航条
[6] **Seller Account**：卖方账户

[7] **comments regarding**：关于……的评价

[8] **via**：[ˈvaiə] prep.（表示方式）通过

You may list items at any price you feel is fair, regardless of the Amazon.com price or **list price.** However, be sure that you take our **commissions and fees** into consideration along with the cost of shipping. Amazon.com provides a fixed shipping credit; however it may not cover your actual shipping cost.

(4) Select shipping method.

You can choose to ship orders to buyers yourself or use Amazon's fulfillment services to do ship for you. If you choose to do ship yourself, decide whether you want to offer **expedited** or international shipping. When you offer a certain shipping option, you can mail your order using any carrier and method, as long as the buyer receives their **package** within the time frame they chose.

If you choose to have Amazon ship orders for you, your listings will **be eligible for** free.

Super Saver Shipping, Prime, customer service, and returns, Fulfillment By Amazon (FBA) fees will apply.

(5) Optional: set Quantity.etc..

(6) Confirm.

**Review** the information you have entered carefully to make sure that your listing will appear as want it to. Although you can edit certain fields in your Seller Account once your listing has been created, other fields, such as "condition", cannot be edited. If you want to change the condition, it will be necessary to close the **current** listing and create another.

Register and Start Selling Today. Please have the following before you begin:

---

[1] **list price**：价目单
[2] **commissions and fees**：佣金和费用

[3] **expedited**：['ekspidaitid] *adj.* 加快的

[4] **package**：['pækidʒ] *n.* 包裹

[5] **be eligible for**：符合……的条件

[6] **Review**：[ri'vju:] *v.* 回顾，检查，检讨，重新考虑

[7] **current**：['kʌrənt] *adj.* 现在的，现行的

- Your business name, address, and **contact information**.
- An **internationally-chargeable** credit card with valid billing address.
- A phone number where you can be reached during this **registration process**.

[1] **contact information**：联系信息

[2] **internationally-chargeable**：国际可支付的

[3] **registration process**：注册流程

Important Notice for International Sellers:
- If you are registering from a country which is outside of the United States, there are important steps you must take before you begin selling on our Amazon.com website to ensure a great experience for you and for customers. These steps include:
- You will have to provide a bank account in the United States in order to be paid.
- You must accurately state the "shipping from" country in your Amazon.com seller profile for display to customers.
- You will be responsible for assuring that you will meet the shipping expectations for all orders you receive.
- You should understand the laws that apply to you as a seller on our website and only list, sell, and export products that **comply with** those laws.

[4] **comply with**：适用于

[1] **obligations**：obligation [ˌɔbliˈgeiʃən] 的复数，n. 义务，责任，职责

Please read this important information for international sellers for more details of your **obligations** as a seller on our website.

If you cannot comply with the requirements of this registration, please do not continue with this registration process.

Select an Option to Begin:

    ◯ Create a new account (**Recommended** for Business accounts).

[2] **Recommended**：recommend [rekəˈmend] 的过去分词形式，v. 推荐，介绍，赞许某人（某事物）

    ◯ Use existing Amazon.com customer account.

...

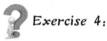  Exercise 4：

Choose the best option and fill in the bracket with the mark No..

1. Amazon.com was sponsored by (　　).

A. Jeff Bezos　　　　　　　　　　B. Lei Jun

C. Pierre Omidyar　　　　　　　　D. TOM

2. Dose Amazon.com charge commissions for seller? (　　)

A. No, it doesn't.

B. Yes, it dose.

C. The commission will be charged after products are sold out.

D. When all products of you are sold out.

3. How many sections can be used to submit product you sell? (　　)

A. One　　　　　　　　　　　　　B. Two

C. Three　　　　　　　　　　　　D. Four

4. When you want to sell items on the Amazon.com, how to price? Which one is not correct? (　　)

A. You can price them according to your situation.

B. Amazon will give you the sole price you may use.

C. You can refer to the price list offered by Amazon.com.

D. You can refer to the same product's price on Amazon.com.

5. The shipping is a very important department in E-commerce, which one of the following is right? (　　)

A. Shipping by Amazon.com is free.

B. Except for the great volume, prime, consumer service and returns, the shipping will be not free.

C. All of them will be charged.

D. Some shipping services are free.

6. Once your listing has been created, you (　　).

A. can edit your condition

B. can't edit any place

C. can edit certain fields

D. needn't to close the listing to edit your conditions

7. Registering for selling on the Amazon.com, some information must be filled in, excluding (　　).

A. Your business name

B. Your address

C. Internationally-chargeable credit card

D. Your home phone number

8. As an international seller, the steps include (　　).

A. a bank account outside America

B. detailed shipping information

C. all orders you receive through Amazon.com

D. your price list

9. Shipping expectations are significant to international sellers, because (　　).

A. it will influnce the frame of your business

B. buyer can get the right item

C. sellers are not very good at business on web

D. we are all the web users

10. What can we infer from the article? (　　)

A. Amazon.com is a website with only one function of selling.

B. People all like to sell products on Amazon .com.

C. International sellers are common on Amazon .com.

D. International shipping is free.

参考译文及答案

# 单元六　网络营销

博客

### 我的网络营销

今天是我暑假的第一天，这个暑假意义深远，我将开始我的兼职工作。我感到非常兴奋，同时又有些紧张。兴奋的是，首先，这个兼职工作是我反复面试后的成果；其次，它是我人生中第一次独立地去进行实习；最后，我的这次实习是我大学专业课程的社会应用，我的工作职责是网络营销，所学的理论知识终于有了实践的机会。感到紧张的是我能否胜任这个工作，是否会给公司带来业绩。不管怎样，我都会勤奋努力地去完成我的各项任务。

我所在的公司在传统方式下也有自己的营销活动，主要是在报纸、公司宣传小册子、展会上等传统途径下宣传自己，现在扩展到网络营销业务，网络营销是伴随互联网的产生而产生的，基本思想是利用互联网为基本手段去营造公司经营环境，是为实现企业总体经营目标所进行的，是企业整体营销战略的一部分。

网络营销和营销的区别是营销的范围更广泛，网络营销的平台是互联网，而营销可以超越互联网的范畴，网络营销是营销的一种而不是唯一的方式。同时网络营销不等于电子商务而是电子商务的一部分。

网络营销的主要功能就是帮助企业树立品牌、进行网站推广、在线销售、信息发布、在线调研、网上促销、巩固顾客关系等。

网络营销的两种主要方法是基于公司网站的营销和无站点营销，基于站点的营销比如戴尔公司自建网站所具有的营销功能，无站点的适用于那些没有自己独立站点的公司，比如个体经营者没有实力建立自身网站的话，可以利用电子商务网站如环球资源网等来做宣传。只需要提供相应广告费用，就可以提高企业在电子商务网站上的可见度，实现营销功能。

网络营销工具各种各样，我喜欢的营销方式有网站营销，搜索引擎比如谷歌、百度等知名引擎营销；电子邮件营销，比如我们可以建立内部列表如公司自己的企业邮箱，利用它来收集电子邮件地址，然后通过这些资源向目标群发送企业营销信息。而外部列表服务商的利用可以实现大量邮件的代发，由于是服务商代表企业来执行这项营销工作，这样企业可以节省时间和精力。博客营销如专业博客平台博客网或者电子商务网站阿里巴巴等博客栏目营销利用。

此外随着 Web 2.0、Web 3.0 技术产生多种网络营销方式。RSS 营销，比如周博通阅读器；论坛营销；即时通信工具，比如 QQ、阿里旺旺、Skype、MSN 等聊天工具营销；电子书营销；微博微信短信营销，阿里巴巴的来往，还有利用无线通信工具如 4G 手机等 WAP 营销方法。

*精读*

## 1997 年与网络营销

对中国人来说，1997 年是不平常的一年，因为香港回归到祖国的怀抱。同样，这一年对商界来说意义重大，因为它是中国网络营销元年。

在 1997 年 2 月，ChinaByte 开通免费新闻邮件服务，到年底，新闻邮件订户数接近 3 万。3 月，在 ChinaByte 网站上又出现了第一个商业性网络广告(468×60 像素标准 banner)。11 月，国内首家专业的网络杂志发行商"索易"开始提供第一份免费网络杂志。这些都标志着网络营销的产生。

当然这只是开创性的几个成果，网络营销的发展也并不是直线上升，直到 2000 年互联网泡沫破灭之后它才开始大幅度发展。因为它使人们从盲目跟风建网站却没有得到什么回报转变过来，开始理性面对互联网，注重它的盈利性发挥，进而刺激了网络营销服务商蓬勃发展。至今，网络营销在企业良好发展的过程中扮演着重要角色。

*泛读*

## 从搜索引擎开始做广告

（部分参考 http://cn.yahoo.com）

搜索引擎是目前比较受欢迎的营销工具之一，因为网民通常都是利用搜索引擎来进行各种各样的信息的搜集的。因此，作为市场营销人员，我们不应该错过这个难得的机会。

那么如何使用搜索引擎进行营销呢？有两种方式。一种模式是我们可以向百度、谷歌等网站免费提交自己的网站域名，我只需打开免费域名提交窗口，在相应位置正确输入域名和验证码，然后单击"提交"按钮即可。另一种方式是参与关键词竞价来进行内容相关的网络广告。这种方式见效快，也比较省心，我可以按照该服务相关服务商的提示一步一步地操作来进行竞价。以雅虎网站为例进行说明。下面几段关于广告的方法来自雅虎网广告栏目。

利用雅虎搜索引擎做广告，只需五步简单操作即可。

(1) 通过地理位置的定位来向你的目标客户展示广告。可以面向全球用户，也可以选择特定的地区或城市。

(2) 选择与你生意相关的关键词。输入你公司提供产品和服务相关的词语或句子。你的公司提供哪些内容？输入那些你希望促销的指定产品或服务。把你自己想象成为一个在网上寻找你公司提供的特定产品和服务的潜在消费者。那么你会去寻找哪些词语？你又会寻找什么产品或服务呢？为了达到最好效果，每一个你描述的产品和服务的关键词都必须精确；它应该是当你的潜在顾客在网上浏览时将会发现的你的公司促销的产品或服务。接下来的例子阐述了你选择的关键词如何紧扣潜在消费者所寻找的产品和服务。"电视"词语很普通；而"等离子平板电视"比较贴切。因此，我将仔细选择自己的关键词，让它充分展示我公司要营销的方向。

不确定自己要输入什么好吗？那就寻找你网站相关的关键词。接下来，输入 50 个关键词或者含关键词的语句。

(3) 告诉雅虎你希望花费多少，详细说明你的每日最少和最高出价。

(4) 创作你的广告内容，编写你将在雅虎上向潜在消费者展示的广告。

(5) 发布广告或者保存广告，检查好你做的广告后输入你的账单信息使广告正式发布，或者保存好广告直到你准备发布为止。看到这，我想，大家差不多都会进行搜索引擎广告了吧。那就让我们自信些，现在就开始为这项营销工作准备吧！

相关链接

**在亚马逊网站进行销售**

（来源：http://www.amazon.com）

建立于1995年的亚马逊网站是世界上领先的电子商务网站，它由贝索斯创建。直到今天这个网站对买卖双方来说，还是世界上著名的站点。

当你想让自己的产品通过亚马逊网站出现在数以亿计的消费者面前时——你的产品将会被亚马逊安排在适当位置展示，直到你的产品卖出去前，是不收任何费用的。

现在就开始，列出你的项目。

(1) 寻找自己打算卖的产品类目。当你找到匹配类目后，单击该页面右边的"在这销售"按钮。注意：同一产品可能有几个版本或格式——确定你的选择是正确的。

你也可以在亚马逊主页上单击"销售你的货物"导航条或者单击在你的销售账户下的管理存货部分，来发布产品。

(2) 描述产品参数。

选择参数并输入相关产品评价。

(3) 注册并设定单价来收集来自销售区域买方的在线支付。

通过亚马逊支付。

你可以设定你认为公平的产品单价，而不用管亚马逊网站上的价目表。然而，要确保你已将包括运费在内我们的承诺和费用考虑在内。亚马逊提供固定的物流信用；但这可能不包含你的实际运费。

(4) 选择物流方式。

你可以选择自己负责物流或者使用亚马逊为你履行的服务。如果你自己负责物流，你要决定是否快递或者进行国际物流。当你选择自己物流时，你可以使用任何一种方式来邮递你的货物，只要买方在规定的时间内收到货物即可。

如果你选择亚马逊为你进行物流服务，你的货物要符合免费服务条件。由亚马逊负责的巨惠、送货、首要送货、顾客服务、退货等则要给亚马逊支付费用。

(5) 备选：设置数量等。

(6) 确认。

仔细检查你输入的信息，确定你的信息如愿显示。你的表单一旦生成，尽管你可以在你的卖方账户特定区域编辑自己的信息，但如"参数"等其他地方是不可以编辑的，如果你想改变条件参数，你将需要关闭当前表单并重新创建。

现在就注册并开始销售。开始前请按照下列要求来做：

- 你公司名称、地址、联系方式。
- 有效地址的国际信息卡。
- 可以随时联系到你的电话。

对国际卖家的重要提醒如下：

- 如果你是美国以外的注册用户，当你在亚马逊网站开始销售产品时，必须严格按照亚马逊网站的步骤来确保你和消费者都是具有丰富网上交易经验的。这些步骤包括：

- 你将需要提供美国银行账号以备收款使用。
- 在亚马逊网站卖方部分你必须准确叙述"起运"国家以便清晰展示给顾客。
- 你将确保对你所接到的每一笔订单的物流承诺负责。
- 你应该了解亚马逊对卖方的法律规范，但只有购货单、产品销售、产品出口适用此法律。

作为亚马逊网站国际卖家，请你仔细阅读这些重要的信息来详细了解你应该承担的义务。如果你不能满足上述注册要求，请不要再继续注册程序。请选择：

○ 创建一个新账户（建议是商业账户）。
○ 使用你已经具有的亚马逊账户。

```
练习一    （略）
练习二    （略）
练习三    （略）
练习四    1. A   2. C   3. C   4. B   5. D   6. C   7. D   8. B   9. A   10. C
```

# Unit Seven

## Network Communication

Blog: Internet Communication

Intensive Reading: Microblogging

Extensive Reading: WeChat

Related Links: Facebook

## Internet Communication

Hello, everybody! Welcome to my Blog! This time we are going to talk about internet communication.

Our society keeps developing, communications between people are becoming more and more frequent. In addition to oral talks and telephone talks, internet communication has become popular in the recent years.

I once **submitted** my homework by E-mail, shared my travel pictures in **cyberspace** and discussed Hollywood movie Avatar with my friends.

That is right! All is internet communication. It has changed our lives!

Internet communication can be realized mainly by E-mail, BBS, Blog, MicroBlog, Internet Telephony, WeChat and etc..

[1] **submitted**：submit [səb'mit] 的过去式，v. 提交，登录

[2] **cyberspace**：['saibəspeis] n. 网络空间

[1] **advantage**: [əd'vɑ:ntidʒ] *n.* 优势，好处，利益，[同义] benefit

[2] **permanent**: ['pə:mənənt] *adj.* 永久的，长久的

[3] **exchange**: [iks'tʃeindʒ] *n.* 交换，兑换

[4] **convenience**: [kən'vi:njəns] *n.* 方便，便利

[5] **delivery**: [di'livəri] *n.* 传递，传送，交货，deliver 的名词形式

[6] **personnel**: [,pə:sə'nel] *n.* 人员，员工，职工，[同义]staff

[7] **forwarding**: forward ['fɔ:wəd] 的 ing 形式，*v.* 转发，运输

[8] **establishment**: [is'tæbliʃmənt] *n.* 建立，设立，机构，[同义] foundation

[9] **continuously**: [kən'tinjuəsli] *adv.* 不断地，连续地，[同义] constantly

[10] **respectively**: [ri'spektivli] *adv.* 分别地，各自地

[11] **forums**: forum ['fɔ:rəm] 的复数，*n.* 论坛，网络论坛

[12] **various**: ['vɛəriəs] *adj.* 不同的，各种的

[13] **consumption**: [kən'sʌmpʃən] *n.* 消费，消费量

[14] **activities**: activity [æk'tiviti] 的复数，*n.* 活动，消遣活动

[15] **considerations**: consideration [kənsidə'reiʃən] 的复数，*n.* 考虑，思考

Internet communication enjoys the **advantage** of low cost. Many services are free, even for **permanent** use. In addition, information **exchange** rate is faster than the traditional manner. Many services can become interactive. Thus it has brought a lot of **convenience** to people's work and life.

E-mail is the widest service applied in internet. It is easy to use with rapid **delivery**. You can put words, images and animation in E-mail. Bill Gates, the founder of Microsoft, has always contacted with his **personnel** by E-mail.

Immediate messages **forwarding** and receiving can be realized between several users through Instant Messaging. Since **establishment** in 1998, Instant Messaging has developed rapidly. Its functions have been **continuously** improving. Such as MSN and Tencent, they have **respectively** had hundreds of millions of users in the world.

BBS allows its users to visit online community and read news, download or upload files and exchange information with other users. Some famous BBS always have a lot of users. In the **forums**, they can discuss on **various** topics involved with learning, life and **consumption**.

As a kind of information publication mode, blog has been rising in recent years. Users can release their **activities**, views, **considerations** and feelings in the specific websites. By blog, information can be shared.

It is a sign of network **popularization**.

Internet telephony refers to voice, **facsimile**, and voicemessaging applications, it is a **feasible** mode of voice communications over internet. Most people think that internet telephony can **sharply** reduce communication and **infrastructure** costs.

Google Talk and Vonage are the main internet telephony service providers. Skype, which originally **marketed** itself as a service among friends, has begun to **cater** to businesses, providing free-of-charge connection between any users.

Finally, I want to say that, during internet communication, some manners should be **remarked**, such as respecting others, using **civilized** words, not **inquiring** upon others' privacy and not making regional discriminations.

Internet communication can make our lives more colorful. My QQ is 12345678. Welcome to communicate with me by QQ!

[1] **popularization**: [ˌpɒpjulərai'zeiʃən] n. 大众化, 通俗化, 普及
[2] **facsimile**: [fæk'siməli] n. 传真, 电传, Fax 传真机
[3] **feasible**: ['fi:zəbl] adj. 可行的, 合理的, [同义] possible
[4] **sharply**: ['ʃɑːpli] adv. 锋利地, 急剧地, 明显地
[5] **infrastructure**: ['infrə'strʌktʃə] n. 基础设施, 基本建设, 公共建设
[6] **marketed**: market ['mɑːkit] 的过去式, v. 推销
[7] **cater**: ['keitə] v. 迎合, 投合, 备办食物

[8] **remarked**: remark [ri'mɑːk] 的过去分词形式, v. 谈到, 谈论, 注意, 评论
[9] **civilized**: ['sivilaizd] adj. 文明的, 有礼貌的, 有教养的, [同义] polite
[10] **inquiring**: inquire [in'kwaiə] 的 ing 形式, v. 查询, 调查

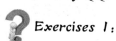

*Exercises 1:*

1. Speaking: List at least 6 methods of internet-communication in English.
2. Writing: Write down your interesting experiences of internet communication in English (50~80 words, including: when/where/who/what topic/ which method).
3. Vocabulary Learning.

| | |
|---|---|
| ① cater | lasting for a long time or for all time in the future |
| ② civilized | that is possible and likely to be achieved |
| ③ permanent | to provide the things that a particular person or situation needs or wants |
| ④ personnel | having or showing polite and reasonable behavior |
| ⑤ feasible | not requiring any payment; without any payment being required |
| ⑥ free-of-charge | the people who work for an organization |

## Notes

(1) internet communication　网络交流，目前常见的交流沟通方式之一。人们可通过电子邮件、即时通信、BBS 等方式在互联网上交流。

(2) oral talks　口语交谈。

例句：Oral Talks in international conference. 在国际会议上口头会谈。

(3) Hollywood　好莱坞，是全球著名的电影城以及娱乐和旅游热门地点，位于美国加利福尼亚州洛杉矶市市区西北郊。

(4) Avatar　《阿凡达》，好莱坞近年拍摄的一部 3D 立体科幻电影，该片投资超过 5 亿美元，全球票房近 25 亿美元，是世界电影史上的票房冠军。

(5) internet telephony　网络电话，即完全通过 internet 传输语音信号，不再通过电信运营商的电话交换网，因而费用极低，甚至免费，但用户端需要安装特定软件或设备。

(6) SNS　全称是 Social Networking Services，即社会性网络服务。

SNS 专指旨在帮助人们建立社会性网络关系的互联网应用服务。在互联网领域 SNS 有三层含义：服务，Social Network Service；软件，Social Network Software；网站，Social Network Site。现在许多 Web 2.0 网站都属于 SNS 网站，如网络聊天(IM)、交友、视频分享、博客、播客、网络社区等。社会性网络的理论基础源于六度分割理论(Six Degrees of Separation)和 150 法则(Rule of 150)。

(7) traditional manner　传统方式。

例句：How to eat SUSHI in Japanese traditional manner? 如何以日本传统方式吃寿司？

(8) (in)contact with 接触，与……有联系；make contact with 与……联系；out of contact with 与……失去联系。

例句：In contact with the right people. 和正当的人来往。

(9) online community 网络社区，网上社区。

例句：Vote for your choice for Best Online Community. 票选你最喜欢的网络社区。

(10) 严格来说，BBS 与 forums(网络论坛)是不同的，由于基于 telnet 连接方式的传统 BBS 日渐衰落，近年来两者正逐渐趋同。

(11) involve with(sb.) 与(某人)有密切关系。

例句：You shouldn't involve yourself with him. 你不该跟他有任何瓜葛。

(12) Google Talk Google 公司开发的即时通信工具，Google Talk 除了具备一般 IM 功能外，还有 VIOP 功能，界面美观大方，可直接链接到 Gmail，轻松接收邮件。

(13) Vonage 2003 年在美国成立，是在美国纽约证券交易所上市的 IP 电话和会话发起协议的网络公司，主要提供基于宽带的电话服务。

(14) Skype 一家全球性互联网电话公司，它通过在全世界范围内向客户提供免费高质量通话服务，正在逐渐改变电信业。Skype 同时也是公司旗下网络即时语音沟通工具的名称。

(15) free of charge 免费。

例句：Please take it, free of charge. 请拿一本去吧，这是免费的。

(16) inquire upon 打听，查询。

例句：Can you help me inquire upon her QQ number? 你能帮我打听她的 QQ 号码吗？

(17) regional discriminations 地域歧视，地域攻击。

例句：Regional discrimination in China due to the scope of human activities are mostly in the same region, the people of other regions are usually not familiar with each other. 中国的地域歧视，主要归因于人们固定生活在一个区域内，不同地区的人通常互不熟悉对方。

## Tips for Translation

(1) I once...and discussed Hollywood movie Avatar with my friends.

在表达"谈论……话题"时，很多人习惯在 discuss 后面使用介词 about，这其实是画蛇添足，因为 discuss = talk about。

(2) low cost 或者 low-cost 低成本；低成本的，廉价的。

例句：Best low-cost bets: mascara, lipstick, and foundation. 最值得买的优价化妆品是：画眉笔、口红和底霜。

(3) Immediate messages forwarding and receiving can be realized between several users through Instant Messaging. 多人之间即时消息的发送和接收可通过即时通信工具来实现。

注意此处 Immediate message 与 Instant Messaging 的意思大不相同。

(4) Internet telephony refers to voice, facsimile, and voice-messaging applications…网络电话涉及语音、传真和语音程序等。

refer to 提及，涉及，关系到。

例句：This is not the book which I referred to. 这不是我所指的那本书。

(5) Skype, which originally marketed itself as a service among friends…

由于 Skype 既是公司名称又是软件名称，在翻译的时候可适当联系上下文，如此翻译较为合适：Skype 公司原来宣称自己的软件主要在私人用户之间使用，现在开始迎合企业……

## Intensive Reading

### Microblogging

Microblogging is a form of blogging. A microblog **differs** from a **traditional** blog in that its content is **typically** much smaller, in both actual size and total file size.

A microblog **entry** could consist of nothing but a short sentence **fragment**, or an image or **embedded** video.

As with traditional blogging, microbloggers post about topics ranging from the simple, such as "what I'm doing right now," to the **thematic**, such as "sports cars." Commercial microblogs also exist, to promote websites, services and/or products.

Some microblogging services offer features such as **privacy** settings, which allow users to control who can read their microblogs, or **alternative** ways of publishing entries besides the web-based interface. These may include text messaging, instant messaging, E-mail, or digital audio.

[1] **differs**: differ [ˈdifə] 的第三人称单数形式, v. 不同, 相异
[2] **traditional**: [trəˈdiʃən(ə)l] adj. 传统的, 惯例的
[3] **typically**: [ˈtipikəli] adv. 作为特色地
[4] **entry**: [ˈentri] n. 入场, 项目, 作品
[5] **fragment**: [ˈfræɡmənt] n. 碎片, 片断
[6] **embedded**: [imˈbedid] adj. 嵌入式的

[7] **thematic**: [θiːˈmætik] n. 专题栏目, [同义] topic/topical

[8] **privacy**: [ˈpraivəsi] n. 隐私
[9] **alternative**: [ɔːlˈtəːnətiv] adj. 非此即彼的, 另一种的, [同义] alternate

[1] **usage**: ['ju:zidʒ] *n.* 使用，用途，[同义]utilization/use

[2] **counted**: count [kaunt] 的过去分词形式，*v.* 计算，[同义]calculate

[3] **notable**: ['nəutəbl] *adj.* 著名的，显著的，[同义]noted

[4] **available**: [ə'veiləbl] *adj.* 可用的，在手边的

[5] **maintain**: [men'tein] *v.* 维持，保持，坚持，[同义]sustain/ retain

[6] **aggregate**: ['ægrigeit] *v.* 使聚集，聚集，[同义]assemble

The first microblogs were known as Tumblelogs. It was built in 2005. However, by 2006 and 2007, the term microblog came into greater **usage** for such services provided by Tumblr and Twitter. In May 2013, 189 microblogging sites were **counted** internationally. Among the most **notable** services are Twitter, Tumblr, Weibo, Èmote.in, Squeelr, Beeing, Jaiku and identi.ca.

Other leading social networking websites Face Book, MySpace, LinkedIn, and XING also have their own microblogging feature, better known as status updates.

Users and organizations are also able to set up their own microblogging service. Open source and free software is **available** for download for this purpose.

With the growth of microblogging, many users want to **maintain** presence in more than one or more social networks. Services such as Lifestream and Profilactic will **aggregate** microblogs from multiple social networks into a single list. Services such as Ping.fm will send out your microblog to multiple social networks.

 *Exercise 2*:

Speaking: What are the differences between Blogging and Microblogging?
Writing: Write down at least 5 Microblogging service providers.

## Notes

(1) microblogging 微博，是一种迷你型博客，可以通过手机、IM 软件(MSN、QQ、Skype)等途径向自己的微博发布即时消息，但每次只能发送不超过 140 个字符的短消息。

(2) differ from 与……不同，区别于。

例句：Chinese differs greatly from English in spelling. 汉语和英语在拼写上大不相同。

(3) consist of 由……构成(组成)；be composed of 由……组成；be comprised of 由……组成。三者意思相近，注意结合下面的例句加以区别。

例句：Water consists of hydrogen and oxygen. 水由氢和氧组成。

Our class is composed of eighteen boys and twelve girls. 我们班由 18 个男生和 12 个女生组成。

This field is comprised of the following parts. 该字段由下列几部分组成。

(4) range from...to... 范围从……至……

例句：Values range from 0 to 256. 取值范围为 0 到 256。

(5) web-based 基于网络的。类似组合词如 text-based，基于文本的。

例句：Construction of web-based BBS. 基于 web 的 BBS 系统的构建。

(6) come into 进来，得到，获得。come into being 形成。

例句：To come into effect. 生效。

(7) Twitter 原意是鸟等发出啁啾声。中文名称"推特"，是目前美国乃至全球范围内著名的社交网络及手机微博网站，它利用无线网络、有线网络、通信技术进行即时通信，是微博的典型应用。它允许用户将自己的最新动态和想法以短信息的形式发

送给手机网站群，而不仅仅是发送给某个人。后面提到的 Tumblr、Weibo、Emote.in、Squeelr、Beeing、Jaiku and identi.ca 都是知名的微博网站。

(8) social networking website　社交网站，是 Social Networking Services(SNS，社会性网络服务)的重要组成部分。

(9) 国内和国外著名的社交网站包括 Facebook、Myspace、Xing.com、人人网(校内网)、开心网等。

Myspace 成立于 2003 年 9 月，是目前全球第二大社交网站，拥有超过 2 亿名注册用户。2005 年 7 月，新闻集团(News Corporation)以 5.8 亿美元现金收购了 MySpace。2006 年年初，Myspace 开始启动其全球化战略，其在国内的网站是 http://www.myspace.cn/。

(10) …better known as status updates　此处做补语成分，主语是那几个网站，指这几个社交网站以资讯更新而闻名。

例句：To the south of San Francisco is the area with a large of number of computer technology companies—better known as Silicon Valley. 旧金山南部地区拥有大量的计算机技术公司，即闻名的硅谷。

(11) open source　开放源码(的程序)。对于一个开放源代码的应用程序来说，允许公众获得该应用程序的源程序代码，并可以对获得的源程序代码进行修改。部分开源软件如 Linux、open office。

 Extensive Reading

## WeChat

(Sources: http://en.wikipedia.org)

WeChat is a mobile text and voice messaging communication service developed by Tencent in China, first **released** in January 2011.

The **app** is available on Android, iPhone, BlackBerry, Windows Phone, and Symbian platforms. Languages supported include traditional/simplified Chinese, English, Spanish, **Portuguese**, Malay, Japanese, Korean, Italian, Thai, and Russian. WeChat is supported on **Wi-Fi**, 2G, 3G, and 4G data networks.

WeChat provides multimedia communication with text messaging, **hold-to-talk** voice messaging, broadcast (one-to-many) messaging, photo/video sharing, location sharing, and contact information exchange. WeChat supports social networking **via** shared **streaming content** feeds and location-based social **plug-ins** ("Shake", "Look Around", and "Drift Bottle") to chat with and connect with local and international WeChat users.

Photos can be taken and **embellished** with artistic **filters**, **captions**, and placed into a personal photo journal for sharing with other users. User data is protected via an on-demand contact list backup and **retrieval** to/from the cloud.

In July 2013, the number of WeChat **oversea** users have **surpassed** 70 million, and Tencent would launch global ad promotion working with football star Lionel Andrés Messi.

[1] **released**: release [riˈliːs] 的过去式, v. 释放, 放开, 发布, 发行

[2] **app**: [æp] n.计算机应用程序, 此处主要指手机应用程序

[3] **Portuguese**: [ˌpɔːtʃuˈgiːz] n. 葡萄牙语

[4] **Wi-Fi**: [ˈwai, fai] 是一种基于IEEE 802.11b 标准的无线局域网

[5] **hold-to-talk**: 按住说话, 是微信提供的一种语音聊天功能

[6] **via**: [ˈvaiə] prep.经过, 通过, 凭借, 取道

[7] **streaming content**: 流媒体内容

[8] **plug-ins**: n.插件

[9] **embellished**: embellish [imˈbeliʃ] 的过去分词形式, v. 装饰; 修饰

[10] **filters**: filter [ˈfiltə(r)] 的复数, n. 滤波器; 滤镜

[11] **captions**: caption [ˈkæpʃn] 的复数, n. 标题, 字幕

[12] **retrieval**: [riˈtriːvl] n. 备份

[13] **oversea**: [ˌəuvəˈsiː] adj. 外国的, 海外的

[14] **surpassed**: surpass [səˈpɑːs] 的过去分词形式, v. 超过, 优于, 胜过

[1] **pre-install**：预装（软件）

[2] **touch-screen**：触摸屏

[3] **sketches**：sketch [sketʃ] 的复数，n. 草图，素描

[4] **selling point**：卖点

[5] **massive**：['mæsiv] adj. 大量的，大块的

WeChat is not the only mobile messaging service in China. Here are a few key competitors of WeiChat.

1. Xiaomi MiTalk

The Xiaomi phone received over 300,000 preorders on it's first day of pre-order sales. MiTalk comes **pre-installed** one each one.

Each MiTalk users has a wall on which friends can post messages. And MiTalk also offers a "doodle pad",so you can send your friends your **touch-screen sketches**.

2. Feixin IM

This is an app by China Mobile. Its biggest **selling point** is free SMS for you and your Feixin friends.

China Mobile is the one other company that approaches Tencent with its control of a **massive** userbase. Let the race begin.

 Exercise 3：

Choose the best option and fill in the bracket with the mark No..

1. Which one is not the major feature of WeChat? (    )
   A. real-time          B. text-based          C. browser-based only          D. based voice
2. WeChat can be used by (    ).
   A. only one person                     B. only two users
   C. between two or more users           D. feature phone users
3. WeChat first appears in (    ).
   A. 2009          B. 2010          C. 2011          D. 2012
4. (    ) is the biggest selling point of Feixin.
   A. Free          B. More users          C. Based computer          D. Free SMS
5. (    ) is the key competitor of WeiChat.
   A. QQ            B. MiTalk              C. SMS                   D. China Mobile
6. Which one is the most popular messaging communication service？(    )
   A. MSN           B. WeChat              C. QQ                    D. sina UC
7. There are about (    ) oversea users of WeChat in July 2013.
   A. 14,000,000    B. 7,000,000           C. 17,000,000            D. 70,000,000

## Tips for Translation

(1) be available on 可用在。

例句：The service will initially be available on only one phone, the new motorola droid.

这项服务最初只能用在最新的摩托罗拉德罗伊德这一款手机上。

(2) Android、iPhone、BlackBerry、Windows Phone、Symbian 是几个主流的手机操作系统（平台），分别来自谷歌、苹果、黑莓、微软、诺基亚等公司。

(3) broadcast，是一种通信方式，一个发送端可同时向多个接收端发送信息。

(4) Shake, Look Around, Drift Bottle 分别是微信的几个主要功能：摇一摇、附近的人和漂流瓶。

(5) place into 放入；发布。

例句：Collect info from my dealers site to place into mine. 从我的经销商网站收集信息到我的地方。

(6) journal 此处主要指个人空间，即微信中的"我的相册"。

(7) contact list 通讯录。

(8) cloud 此处指云计算系统。

(9) ad promotion 广告推广。

(10) Xiaomi 小米公司，是中国一家著名的智能手机供应商。

(11) selling point 卖点。

例句：Personalisation of applications is also an important selling point online.

个性化应用也是互联网上的一个重要卖点。

(12) SMS（Short Messaging Service）短信息服务，即短信。

(13) userbase 用户基数，用户群体。

例句：Mark Zuckerberg predicts the site's userbase might even reach one billion.

马克·扎克伯格预言该网站的用户群体将达到 10 亿。

(14) Let the race begin 让比赛开始。

例句：Start your engines and let the motorcycle race begin. 发动引擎，让赛车比赛开始吧。

(15) feature phone 功能手机，区别于目前的智能手机 smart phone。

 **Related Links**

## Facebook

(Sources: http://en.wikipedia.org)

 **Facebook** is a social networking website that is operated and privately owned by Facebook Inc. Users can add friends and send them messages, and update their personal **profiles** to notify friends about themselves. Additionally, users can join networks organized by city, workplace, and school or college. The website's name **stems** from the **colloquial** name of books given at the start of the **academic** year by university administrations with the **intention** of helping students to get to know each other better.

Mark Zuckerberg founded Facebook with his college roommates and **fellow** computer science students Eduardo Saverin, Dustin Moskovitz and Chris Hughes while he was a student at Harvard University. The website's **membership** was initially limited by the founders to Harvard students, but was expanded to other colleges in the Boston area, **the Ivy League**, and **Stanford University**. It later expanded further to include (**potentially**) any university student, then high school students,

---

[1] **Facebook**：中文称脸谱，是目前全球最大的社交网站

[2] **profiles**：profile ['prəufail] 的复数，n. 侧面，侧影，简介

[3] **stems**：stem [stem] 的第三人称单数形式，v. 起源于

[4] **colloquial**：[kə'ləukwiəl] adj. 口语的，口头上的

[5] **academic**：[,ækə'demik] adj. 大学的，学院的

[6] **intention**：[in'tenʃən] n. 意图，目的，[同义] purpose/aim

[7] **fellow**：['feləu] n. 伙伴，家伙，研究员，[同义] companion

[8] **membership**：['membəʃip] n. 会员，成员，全体会员

[9] **the Ivy League**：常青藤联盟。由美国东海岸八所著名大学组成，这些大学都有古色古香的建筑物，建筑物的墙壁上爬满了常青藤，故称常青藤联盟。八校分别是：布朗大学、哥伦比亚大学、康奈尔大学、达特茅斯学院、哈佛大学、宾夕法尼亚大学、普林斯顿大学、耶鲁大学

[10] **Stanford University**：斯坦福大学，美国名校，位于美国西海岸的加利福尼亚州

[11] **potentially**：[pə'tenʃ(ə)li] adv. 潜在地，可能地

and, finally, to anyone aged 13 and over. The website currently has more than 1.1 billion active users worldwide.

In Facebook, users can create profiles with photos, lists of personal interests, contact information and other personal information. Communicating with friends and other users can be done through private or public messages or a chat feature. Users can also create and join interest and fan groups, some of which are maintained by organizations **as a means of** advertising. To **combat** privacy **concerns**, Facebook enables users to choose their own privacy settings and choose who can see what parts of their profile.

Facebook has a number of features with which users may interact. They include **the Wall**, a space on every user's profile page that allows friends to post messages for the user to see; **Pokes**, which allows users to send a virtual "poke" to each other (a notification then tells a user that they have been poked); Photos, where users can upload **albums** and photos; and Status, which allows users to inform their friends of their **whereabouts** and actions. Depending on privacy settings, anyone who can see a user's profile can also view that user's Wall.

One of the most popular applications on Facebook is the Photos application, where users can upload albums and photos. Facebook allows users to upload an **unlimited** number of photos, **compared with** other image hosting services such as Photobucket and Flickr, which apply limits to the number of photos that a user is

[1] **as a means of:** 作为……的一种手段
[2] **combat:** ['kɔmbət] v. 消除
[3] **concerns:** concern [kən'sə:n] 的复数, n. 问题

[4] **the Wall:** 涂鸦墙，类似用户页面上的留言板，与留言板不同的是，涂鸦墙的内容会被同步到各个朋友的首页
[5] **Pokes:** 戳，是用户和朋友交互的一种方式

[6] **albums:** album ['ælbəm] 的复数, n. 相册，音乐册

[7] **whereabouts:** ['(h)wɛərə'bauts] n. 行踪，下落，在哪里

[8] **unlimited:** [ʌn'limitid] adj. 无限制的，[同义]limitless/infinite
[9] **compared with:** 与……比较，与……相比

allowed to upload. During the first years, Facebook users were limited to 60 photos per album. As of May 2009, this limit has been increased to 200 photos per album. Privacy settings can be set for **individual** albums, limiting the groups of users that can see an album. For example, the privacy of an album can be set so that only the user's friends can see the album, while the privacy of another album can be set so that all Facebook users can see it.

Facebook launched **Gifts** on February 8, 2007, which allows users to send virtual gifts to their friends that appear on the **recipient**'s profile. Gifts cost $1.00 each to purchase, and a personalized message can be **attached** to each gift. On May 14, 2007, Facebook launched Marketplace, which lets users post free **classified ads**.

According to **Alexa**, the website's **ranking** among all websites increased from 60th to 7th in terms of worldwide **traffic**, from September 2006 to September 2007, and is currently 2nd. **Quantcast** ranks the website 2th in the U.S. in terms of traffic, and **Compete.com** ranks it 1st in the U.S. The website is the most popular for uploading photos, with 30 million uploaded daily.

[1] **individual**: [ˌindiˈvidjuəl] adj. 个人的，个体的，[同义]personal/private

[2] **Gifts**：礼物，用户注册时可免费获得 1 个礼物，以后每个礼物 1 美元。此项收入的 50%捐献给 Susan G. Komen 乳腺癌基金会

[3] **recipient**：[riˈsipiənt] n. 接受者，受领者

[4] **attached**：attach [əˈtætʃ] 的过去分词形式，v. 系上，装上，贴上

[5] **classified ads**：分类广告

[6] **Alexa**：一家专门发布网站世界排名的权威网站

[7] **ranking**：[ˈræŋkiŋ] n. 排名，排位，级别

[8] **traffic**：[ˈtræfik] n. 交通，运输，此处专指网站访问量

[9] **Quantcast**：一家创新型网络公司

[10] **Compete.com**：一家网站及搜索引擎数据分析公司

## Exercise 4:

Choose the best option and fill in the bracket with the mark No..

1. Only (    ) can join the Facebook website initially.

A. Zuckerberg and his friends

B. Harvard students

C. The students of Stanford

D. All the students in the Boston area

2. What is the meaning of "active users" ? (    )

A. all the users

B. the charismatic users

C. the founders of website

D. the people who access the site frequently

3. Which one is not the interactive feature on Facebook? (    )

A. The Wall                           B. Pokes

C. Status                             D. Download

4. What is the most popular application on Facebook? (    )

A. Instant messengers

B. E-mail client

C. Photos application

D. Download application

5. Which option is wrong about Gifts on Facebook? (    )

A. All the gifts are virtual

B. Gifts were launched on February 8, 2007

C. Personal message can be attached to a gift

D. Each gift cost $1.00

6. Now Facebook website's ranking is (    ) in terms of worldwide traffic according to Alexa.

A. 7th                                B. 1st

C. 4th                                D. 2nd

## 参考译文及答案

# 单元七　网络交流

**博客**

### 网络交流

大家好，欢迎来到我的博客，这次我们来谈一谈网络交流。

我们的社会在不断发展，人与人之间的交流越来越频繁，除了原来的口头交谈、打电话，最近几年，网络交流受到了人们的欢迎。

我曾经使用电子邮件提交我的课外作业，在网络空间上分享我的旅游照片，在 BBS 上与朋友讨论阿凡达……

对，这都属于网络交流，它已经改变了我们的生活。

网络交流的主要方式有：电子邮件、即时通信、BBS、博客、微博、网络电话、微信等。

网络交流的优势是成本低，很多服务即使长久使用也是免费的，而且信息交换速度也比传统方式快，很多服务可实现互动。由此它给人们的工作和生活带来了便利。

电子邮件是 Internet 上应用最广的服务，它使用简易、投递迅速。你可以在电子邮件中添加文字、图像、动画资料。微软公司的总裁比尔·盖茨一直利用电子邮件与下属保持联系。

即时通信能够在多个用户之间即时发送和接收消息。自 1998 年诞生以来，即时通信发展非常迅速，它的功能不断丰富。像 MSN 和 Tencent，分别在全球拥有数亿的用户。

BBS 允许用户访问网络论坛，从而阅读新闻，下载或上传文件，与其他用户交换信息。一些著名的网络论坛往往拥有大量的用户，讨论各种各样的话题，包括学习、生活、消费。

作为一种信息发布模式，博客在这几年逐渐兴起，用户可以在专门的网站上发布自己的行动、观点、思考和感想，实现信息分享。博客是网络平民化的一个标志。

网络电话涉及语音、传真和语音程序，它是互联网语音通信的一个可行模式。大多数人认为网络电话可以大大降低通信和基础设施成本。

Google Talk 和 Vonage 公司是主要的网络电话服务商。Skype 公司原来宣称自己的软件主要在私人用户之间使用，现在已经开始迎合企业，在任何用户之间提供免费的连接。

最后，我想告诉大家，在网络交流中需要注意一些礼仪，比如尊重别人、不说脏话，不要打听他人的隐私，不要搞地域攻击。

网络交流可以使我们的生活更精彩。我的 QQ 号码是 12345678，欢迎大家与我通过 QQ 交流。

**精读**

### 微博

微博是博客的一种形式，微博有别于传统的博客，因为其内容通常要小得多，无论是实际大小还是文件大小。

微博可以包括的内容只不过是一句简短的话，或一幅图片或一段嵌入视频。

与传统的博客相比，微博用户张贴的主题包括从简单的内容，如"我现在在做什么"，到一个专题，如"跑车"。商业微博也存在，像网站推广、服务或产品。

有些微博服务商提供了一些功能，如隐私设置，允许用户控制谁可以阅读他们的微博，或者除了基于 web 界面，用户还可选择其他方式在网上发布信息。这些信息可能包括短信、即时消息、电子邮件或数字音频。

Tumblelogs 被称为世界上第一家微博。它建于 2005 年。然而 2006 年和 2007 年，由于 Tumblr 和 Twitter 提供这种服务，微博这个字眼得到了更广泛的使用。2013 年 5 月，根据全球统计共有 189 个微博网站。其中最著名的微博服务商是 Twitter、Tumblr、Plurk、Emote.in、Squeelr、Beeing、Jaiku 和 identi.ca。

其他领先的社交网站 Facebook、MySpace、LinkedIn，以及 XING 也有自己的微博功能，这些网站以更快的资讯信息更新而闻名。

用户和组织也可以建立自己的微博服务。为实现此目的，相关开源代码和免费软件可供用户下载。

随着微博的发展，许多用户希望同时维护一个或多个已注册的社交网络。如 Lifestream 和 Profilactic 提供的服务，可将多个社交网络中的微博聚合到一个单一的列表中。像 Ping.fm 提供的服务将会把你更新的微博信息发送到多个社交网站中。

泛读

## 微信

（来源：http://en.wikipedia.org）

微信是中国的腾讯公司于 2011 年 1 月首次发布的一款手机文本、语音信息交流的服务软件。

微信支持安卓、苹果、黑莓，以及 Windows Phone、塞班等平台。微信可以支持多种语言，包括简繁体中文、英语、西班牙语、葡萄牙语、马来语、日语、韩语、意大利语、泰语、俄语等。微信支持 Wi-Fi、2G、3G 和 4G 等移动数据网络。

微信提供文字消息、语音消息聊天、广播（一对多）消息、照片/视频共享、位置共享，以及通信信息交换等多媒体通信方式。微信支持网络社交，通过流媒体内容分享、基于位置的社交服务，以及"摇一摇""查找附近的人""漂流瓶"等手机插件，用户可与本地和互联网上的微信用户交谈。

用户可利用微信的艺术滤镜、字幕功能来拍摄和装饰照片，并发送到个人照片日志，以分享给其他人。与各用户的交流数据可按需通过联系人列表在云端备份和恢复，以得到保护。

到 2013 年 7 月，微信海外用户已达 7000 万，腾讯还将与足球明星梅西一起开展全球广告推广活动。

在中国，微信不是唯一的手机信息服务软件。下面是微信的几个主要竞争对手。

1. 小米公司的米聊

在预售活动的第一天，小米公司收到了超过 300 000 用户的预订，这些手机中都预装了米聊软件。

每个米聊用户都拥有一个朋友可以张贴信息的留言墙。米聊还提供了一个"涂鸦板"，所以用户可以将自己触摸屏上的草图发给朋友。

2. 飞信

飞信是一款由中国移动公司推出的手机应用,其最大的卖点就是可以给自己及自己的朋友免费发送手机短信。

中国移动公司凭借其掌控的庞大的用户群体,是唯一一个规模与腾讯接近的公司。好戏刚刚开始。

相关链接

## Facebook

(来源:http://en.wikipedia.org)

Facebook是一个社交网站,网站由Facebook公司拥有和独立经营。在网站上用户可以增加朋友和发送消息,并且更新他们的个人档案,通知自己的朋友。此外,用户可以参加由城市、工作地、学校或学院组织的社交网络。该网站的名称源于一本书的通俗叫法,这就是各大学管理机构在每学年年初下发的,用于帮助学生更好地相互了解的花名册。

当创始人马克·扎克伯格还是哈佛大学学生的时候,与自己的大学室友、伙伴,计算机科学专业的爱德华多·萨瓦林、达斯汀·莫斯科维茨和克里斯·休斯一起创办了Facebook网站。该网站的成员最初由创办者限定于哈佛大学的学生,但随后扩展到了在波士顿地区的其他高校,常青藤联盟,以及斯坦福大学。后来进一步扩大到包括(潜在的)任何大学的学生,然后是高中学生,并最终涵盖任何13岁以上的人。该网站目前拥有超过11亿的全球活跃用户。

在Facebook网站上,用户可以创建带有照片的档案,列出个人爱好、联系信息和其他个人资料。与朋友和其他用户沟通可以通过私人或公共的邮件或聊天功能。用户还可以创建和加入兴趣和粉丝群体,其中有些是作为一种广告手段由一些组织维持。为了消除隐私问题,Facebook的用户可以选择自己的隐私设置,选择谁可以看到他们的哪部分文件。

Facebook拥有很多让用户可以互动的功能。这包括"涂鸦墙",在每个用户的配置页面上都有这样一块地方,让朋友可以向用户发送信息让他阅读;"戳"功能,它允许用户相互发送一个虚拟的"戳"给对方(类似一个通知并且告诉用户,他们已接收到其他用户的戳);照片,用户可以上传相册和照片;以及状态,它允许用户告知朋友自己现在在哪里、做什么。根据隐私设置,任何能够看到用户配置文件的人还能够查看该用户的涂鸦墙。

在Facebook上最流行的应用程序之一是照片程序,用户可以上传相册和照片。Facebook允许用户上传无限量的照片,相对于其他图片主机服务商,如Photobucket和Flickr,他们允许用户上传限制数量的照片。在最初几年里,Facebook用户在每个网络相册里只能放60张照片。截至2009年5月,这一限制已经增加到200张照片。个人相册里可以进行隐私设置,以限制某些用户组访问一个相册。例如,某个相册的隐私权可以设定为只允许用户的朋友浏览,而另一个相册可以设定为让所有的Facebook用户都可以浏览。

2007年2月8日,Facebook推出了"礼物"功能,它允许用户发送虚拟礼物给他们的朋友,礼物放置在收件人的文件夹里。每个礼物的购买价格是1美元,在上面可以附加个性化信息。2007年5月14日,Facebook推出了"市场"功能,它允许用户发布免费的分类广告。

据Alexa统计,自2006年9月至2007年9月间,根据全球访问量,该网站在所有网站中的排名由第60名上升至第7名,目前排名第二。依据Quantcast网站排名,按流量计算 Facebook 在美国排名第二，而按照 Compete.com 给出的排名，Facebook 在美国排名第一。Facebook 网站是最流行的分享照片的网站，每天上传的照片为 3000 万张。

练习一
1. E-mail、Instant Messaging、BBS、Blog、Internet telephony、MicroBlog
2. （略）
3. ③-⑤-①-②-⑥-④

练习二
1. Microblogging's content is much smaller than blogging.
The entry of Microblogging is always a short sentence, an image or a short video.
The topic of Microblogging is always about "what I'm doing right now".
In traditional blog, users can write a long article. They can write their views, actions, feelings, and whatever their want.
2. Twitter、Facebook、Beeing、Ping.fm、Sina、Netease

练习三　1. C　2. C　3. C　4. D　5. B　6. B　7. D

练习四　1. B　2. D　3. D　4. C　5. D　6. D

# Unit Eight
## Trade Terms

Blog: Price Terms

Intensive Reading: Why Prices Are So Different in International Trade?

Extensive Reading: Insurance

Related Links: Aliexpress, Escrow and Alipay

## Price Terms

After my store won some success on Net, I heard that some people have begun to do international trade through some platforms on the Internet, such as Alibaba, **global sources** and etc.. After the **financial crisis**, more and more buyers become cautious when they are **placing orders with** sellers, their ordering are turning to the type of **more times, less quantity**.

At the same time, Alibaba found the tendency, and launched **Aliexpress accordingly**. Aliexpress is the platform for sellers to sell commodities directly to the international buyers, which is similar to Taobao, but for international trade not domestic trade.

I am interested in selling my commodities **via** couriers to foreign buyers, but I have to know **Price Terms** before I **quote** prices to buyers. For the price quotation in international trade is completely different from that in domestic trade.

[1] **global sources**：环球资源（网站名）
[2] **financial crisis**：金融危机
[3] **placing orders with**：给……下订单
[4] **more times**：更多次数
[5] **less quantity**：更少数量
[6] **Aliexpress**： *n.* 阿里速卖通
[7] **accordingly**：[əˈkɔːdiŋli] *adv.* 相应地
[8] **via**：[ˈvaiə] *prep.* 经由
[9] **Price Terms**：价格术语
[10] **quote**：[kwəut] *v.* 报价

I remembered I have learned some trade terms in class. **FOB**, **CFR** and **CIF** are the 3 basic price terms

[11] **FOB**：*abbr.* 装运港船上交货价
[12] **CFR**：*abbr.* 成本及运费价
[13] **CIF**：*abbr.* 成本、运费及保险价

used most **frequently** in international trade. To master them is a must to start!

FOB means **Free On Board**, the meaning is that the price includes all the expenses and profits for sellers to transport the **cargo** to the deck of the carrying tool in the **port of loading**.

CFR means **Cost** and **Freight**, the meaning is that the price includes all the expenses and profits for sellers to transport the cargo to **port of discharge** on the carrying tool.

CIF means Cost, Freight and **Insurance**, the meaning is that the price includes all the expenses and profits for sellers to transport the cargo to port of discharge on the carrying tool, and the insurance as well.

The main transportation modes are by truck, train, sea, air post and **pipeline**. The freight will differ a lot from one to another, and it will affect the price finally. The major transportation method for international trade through E-commerce is by **express**. Of course, the freight will be added into the price **no matter** how sellers transport the cargo to buyers.

---

[1] **frequently**: [ˈfriːkwəntli] *adv.* 频繁地

[2] **Free On Board**: 装运港船上交货价

[3] **cargo**: [ˈkɑːgəu] *n.* 货物
[4] **port of loading**: 装运港

[5] **Cost**: [kɔst] *n.* 成本
[6] **Freight**: [freit] *n.* 运费

[7] **port of discharge**: 卸货港

[8] **Insurance**: [inˈʃuərəns] *n.* 保险

[9] **pipeline**: [ˈpaipˌlain] *n.* 管道

[10] **express**: [iksˈpres] *n.* 快递
[11] **no matter**: *conj.* 无论

The insurance are normally three types in international trade, **FPA, WPA** and **AR**.

FPA means **Free** from **Particular Average**, WPA means **With** Particular Average, AR means **All Risks.**

To **cover** FPA, the insurance **rate** is about 3‰ of the 110% **value** of the CIF price, 4‰ for WPA, and 5‰ for AR. The added 10% is for the **predicted profit** of buyers. The most popular **insuring** way is to pay 5‰ of the 110% value of the CIF price **against** AR by sellers, then add the insurance fee to the price.

So, CIF price is higher than CFR price, CFR price is higher than FOB price.

[1] **FPA**：*abbr.* 平安险
[2] **WPA**：*abbr.* 水渍险
[3] **AR**：*abbr.* 一切险
[4] **Free**：*adj.* 免除
[5] **Particular**：*adj.* 特定的
[6] **Average**：*n.* 风险
[7] **With**：*prep.* 带有
[8] **All**：*adj.* 一切的
[9] **Risks**：*n.* 风险
[10] **cover**：[ˈkʌvə] *v.* 投保
[11] **rate**：[reit] *n.* 费率
[12] **value**：[ˈvælju:] *n.* 价值
[13] **predicted profit**：预期利润
[14] **insuring**：投保
[15] **against**：[əˈgenst, əˈgeinst] *prep.* 抵抗

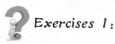

Exercises 1：

Speaking: Make an oral quotation with the price terms to your classmates in English, the quotation should include 4 parts of commodity name, price term, currency unit and measurement unit(50~80 words). For example, leather shoes at USD2.20/PR, FOB Ningbo.

Writing: Write down at least 6 prices for the commodities you are selling internationally on Net in English(50~80 words).

### Notes

(1) Global Sources 国际知名的电子商务平台,与 Alibaba 类似,主要为买卖双方(B2B)提供信息对接服务。

(2) Aliexpress 阿里巴巴旗下跨境小额贸易平台——速卖通,被业内称为淘宝外贸版,主要提供小额在线国际零售业务,通过快递实现物流。卖方可以免费注册,向卖方收取货款的 3%~5% 作为其盈利模式。

(3) Price Terms 价格术语,又称贸易术语(Trade Terms),是进出口商品价格的一个重要组成部分。它是用一个简短的概念或 3 个英语字母的缩写,来说明交货地点、商品的价格构成和买卖双方有关费用、风险和责任的划分,确定卖方交货和买方接货应尽的义务。

(4) quote 名词形式是 quotation,是在国际贸易中专业的表示报价的单词,常见形式有 we quote you the price at…、my quotation is…等。

(5) FOB、CFR 及 CIF 国际贸易 13 种价格术语中最常见的 3 种价格术语,占国际贸易价格术语使用的 80% 以上。具体 13 种价格术语的含义见下页表 8-1(注:实际使用中运输方式及交货地点不限于表中所示)。

(6) FPA、WPA 及 AR 国际贸易中最常用的 3 种基本险别,其翻译是习惯的讲法。其英文原意分别是"单独海损不赔""单独海损也赔""单独海损、共同海损,再加一般一切外来风险都赔",一般的费率分别是 3‰、4‰ 和 5‰。在成交金额不是很大的情况下,由于保费相差不大,所以大都采用以 5‰ 费率投保一切险的方法投保。

表 8-1　国际贸易术语一览表

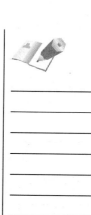

| 组别 | 性质 | 国际代码 | 含义 | | 交货地点 | 运输方式 |
|---|---|---|---|---|---|---|
| | | | 英文 | 中文 | | |
| E 组 | 启运术语 | EXW | Ex Works | 工厂交货 | 商品所在地 | 任何 |
| F 组 | 主运费未付术语 | FCA | Free Carrier | 货交承运人 | 出口国指定地点 | 任何 |
| | | FAS | Free Alongside Ship | 装运港船边交货 | 装运港船边 | 水上 |
| | | FOB | Free on Board | 装运港船上交货 | 装运港船上 | 水上 |
| C 组 | 主运费已付术语 | CFR | Cost and Freight | 成本加运费 | 装运港船上 | 水上 |
| | | CIF | Cost Insurance and Freight | 成本加保险费、运费 | 装运港船上 | 水上 |
| | | CPT | Carriage Paid to | 运费付至 | 出口国指定地点 | 任何 |
| | | CIP | Carriage and Insurance Paid to | 运费、保险费付至 | 出口国指定地点 | 任何 |
| D 组 | 到达术语 | DAF | Delivered at Frontier | 边境交货 | 两国边境指定地点 | 任何 |
| | | DES | Delivered Ex Ship | 目的港船上交货 | 目的港 | 水上 |
| | | DEQ | Delivered Ex Quay | 目的港码头交货 | 目的港码头 | 水上 |
| | | DDU | Delivered Duty Unpaid | 未完税交货 | 进口国指定地点 | 任何 |
| | | DDP | Delivered Duty Paid | 完税后交货 | 进口国指定地点 | 任何 |

(7) predicted profit　预期利润是指如果交易顺利完成，买方预计可以获得的利润。国际贸易的惯例是保险金额在 CIF 价值基础上加成 10% 即 CIF 价值的 110%，在此基础上计算保费。

## Tips for Translation

(1) 当我们翻译英语中的一些价格术语时，除了上述正式准确的翻译以外，还有一些俗称的翻译，比如"FOB"翻译成"离岸价"，"CFR"翻译成"到岸价"，"CIF"翻译成"到岸价(含保险)"。这些翻译不是很精确，但是在口语中也经常使用。

(2) Aliexpress 翻译成阿里速卖通，是阿里巴巴旗下贸易平台。ALI 是阿里巴巴公司的简称，express 的本意是快速。这样的翻译简单明了地表达出这个平台的特性。但就 aliexpress 这个英语单词而言，也是一个新的造词。许多公司采用的商标都是新造词，比如联想 lenovo、比亚迪 BYD(Build Your Dreams)、TCL(Today China Lion)。

(3) port of discharge 卸货港。这样的表达翻译时要倒过来，因为 discharge 是 port 的定语。类似的还有 Bill of Lading (B/L)，提单。英语中的 of 表示"前者属于后者"即要译成"后者(的)前者"，比如"name of the hotel"译为"那家酒店的名称"。

(4) carrying tool 运载工具。"v.+ing"形式做定语，表示所修饰词语的功能。比如"writing pen"表示写字笔。carry 的名词形式 carrier 表示承运人，shipper(consignor) 表示托运人，consignee 表示收货人，构成运输的三方。

(5) predicted profit 预期利润。"v.+ed"形式做定语，表示所修饰词语的来源。predict 是预测的动词原形，而 profit(利润) 是被预测的，所以预期利润就是 predicted profit，相当于"profit which can be predicted"。

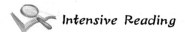 Intensive Reading

## Why Prices Are So Different in International Trade?

In international trade, prices are completely different from domestic trade. FOB, CFR and CIF are the 3 most popular price terms. And we also want to know why they are so different? In order to look into the reasons for the difference between the 3 **above-mentioned** prices, we have to **analyze** the **composition** of them.

FOB=**purchasing cost** (or **manufacturing expense**) + **domestic expense**+**net profit**. Purchasing cost is for **traders** and manufacturing expenses is for **manufacturers**, net profit is for both.

CFR=purchasing cost (or manufacturing expense)+ domestic expense+**foreign freight**+net profit. In this price term, sellers will pay foreign freight for cargo transporttation and then add the cost to the final price. It means CFR price will normally be higher than FOB price, because CFR price includes the foreign freight but FOB price doesn't.

CIF=purchasing cost (or manufacturing expense)+ domestic expense+foreign freight+**foreign insurance fee**+ net profit. It means the CIF price is higher than CFR price, because sellers must pay foreign insurance fee under CIF price term while they don't need to pay that under CFR price term.

So CIF price **goes the highest** among them, CFR price **ranks** the **second** and FOB price **comes the lowest**.

[1] **above-mentioned**：adj. 上述的
[2] **analyze**：['ænəlaiz] v. 分析
[3] **composition**：[kɔmpə'ziʃən] n. 构成
[4] **purchasing cost**：采购成本
[5] **manufacturing expense**：制造费用
[6] **domestic expense**：国内费用
[7] **net profit**：净利润
[8] **traders**：贸易商
[9] **manufacturers**：制造商
[10] **foreign freight**：国外运费

[11] **foreign insurance fee**：国外保险费

[12] **goes the highest**：排名最贵
[13] **ranks the second**：位居第二
[14] **comes the lowest**：处于最低

 Exercise 2：

List at least 5 famous online international trade platforms in English.

## Notes

(1) purchasing cost  采购成本是对贸易商而言的，是指他们为采购商品而支付的费用。

(2) manufacturing expense  制造费用是对制造商而言的，是指他们为生产商品而花费的费用。

(3) foreign freight  国外运费，在我国也指境外运费，是指离开我国装运港(地)的运费，在我国称境外运费更为准确。

(4) domestic expense  国内包含商品在出口之前的一切费用，包括制造、包装、运输、储存、检验及报关等费用。

(5) net profit  出口商(制造商或贸易商)的净利润，是指毛利润(收入中扣除采购成本或制造费用后的余额)减除一切费用后的余额。毛利润称为 gross profit。

(6) foreign insurance  国外保险费。insurance 是保险的名词形式，其动词形式是 insure，为保险而向保险公司支付的保险费是 insurance fee，保费占保险金额的比重称为费率，即 rate。投保也可以用 cover 来表示。

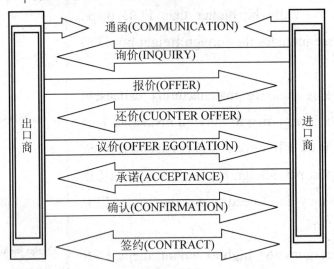

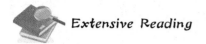
### Extensive Reading

## Insurance

Insurance is to prevent the risks from some **uncertain** and **unpredictable** risks. The **party** who needs insurance services is called "**the insured**", and the party who offers insurance is called "**insurer**". For example, if a **shipper** sends the **cargo** to a **consignee**, the consignee asks the shipper to cover the insurance, then the party who covers the insurance will be the insured, and the insurance company will be the insurer.

The insurer will **be responsible for** some **compensation** according to the **average** the insured covers. The risks are divided into 2 kinds: **perils of the sea**, and **extraneous risks**.

The perils of the sea include **natural disasters** and **accidents**. The natural disasters here only refer to **Force Majeure** such as **heavy weather**, **lightening**, **tsunami**, **earthquake**, **volcanic eruption** and etc.. The accidents here only refer to the **occasional and unexpected** ones such as **grounding, stranding, sunk, collision, missing, fire, explosion** and etc.. The extraneous risks are divided into 2 types: **normal** and **special**. The normal ones include **theft or pilferage, shortage in weight, contamination, leakage, breakage, sweating and/or heating, taint of odour, rusting, hook damage, fresh and/or rain water damage, short-delivery and nondelivery, clashing** and etc.. The special ones include **war, strike, policy** and etc..

[1] **uncertain**: [ʌnˈsəːtn] *adj.* 不确定
[2] **unpredictable**: *adj.* 不可预知的
[3] **party**: [ˈpɑːti] *n.* 一方
[4] **the insured**: *n.* 被保险人
[5] **insurer**: [inˈʃuərə] *n.* 保险人
[6] **shipper**: [ˈʃipə] *n.* 发货人
[7] **cargo**: [ˈkɑːɡəu] *n.* 货物
[8] **consignee**: [kɔnsaiˈniː] *n.* 收货人
[9] **be responsible for**: 负责
[10] **compensation**: [kɔmpenˈseiʃən] *n.* 赔偿
[11] **average**: *n.* 海损
[12] **perils of the sea**: *n.* 海上风险
[13] **extraneous risks**: *n.* 外来风险
[14] **natural disasters**: 自然灾害
[15] **accidents**: *n.* 意外事故
[16] **Force Majeure**: 不可抗力
[17] **heavy weather**: 恶劣天气
[18] **lightening**: 雷电
[19] **tsunami**: 海啸
[20] **earthquake**: 地震
[21] **volcanic eruption**: 火山爆发
[22] **occasional and unexpected**: 偶然且意料之外的
[23] **grounding**: *n.* 搁浅
[24] **stranding**: *n.* 触礁
[25] **sunk**: *n.* 沉没
[26] **collision**: *n.* 碰撞
[27] **missing**: *n.* 失踪
[28] **fire**: *n.* 失火
[29] **explosion**: *n.* 爆炸
[30] **normal**: *adj.* 一般
[31] **special**: *adj.* 特殊
[32] **theft or pilferage**: 偷窃
[33] **shortage in weight**: 短量
[34] **contamination**: *n.* 沾污
[35] **leakage**: *n.* 泄漏
[36] **breakage**: *n.* 破碎
[37] **sweating and/or heating**: 受热受潮
[38] **taint of odour**: 串味
[39] **rusting**: 生锈
[40] **hook damage**: 钩损
[41] **fresh and/or rain water damage**: 淡水雨淋
[42] **short-delivery and nondelivery**: 短少和提货不着
[43] **clashing**: 破损
[44] **war**: *n.* 战争
[45] **strike**: *n.* 罢工
[46] **policy**: *n.* 政策

[1] **total loss**：全部损失
[2] **partial loss**：部分损失
[3] **actual total loss**：实际全损
[4] **constructive total loss**：推定全损
[5] **general average**：共同海损
[6] **particular average**：部分海损

The loss is also divided into 2 kinds: **total loss** and **partial loss**. And among total loss, **actual total loss** and **constructive total loss**. Among partial loss, **general average** and **particular average**.

FPA is possible to be responsible for general average only; WPA is possible to be responsible for general average and particular average both; AR is possible to be responsible for general average, particular average and normal extraneous risks. Though the name is All Risks, but it is not actually responsible for all risks.

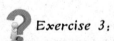 *Exercise 3*:

List some advantages of online trade in English.

For example: convenient.

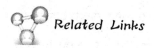

**Related Links**

## Aliexpress, Escrow and Alipay

(Sources: http://help.aliexpress.com/newuserguide;
http://escrow.aliexpress.com/escrow-features/what-is-escrow.html;
https://www.alipay.com/static/aboutalipay/englishabout.htm)

Aliexpress is a new **wholesale marketplace** from Alibaba.com offering wholesale prices on even the smallest **orders**. With **minimum** orders as low as 1 item, secure **escrow** payment, and express **delivery** with full **tracking**, Aliexpress really is your **one-stop-shop**!

[1] **wholesale**：['həulseil] *n.* 批发
[2] **marketplace**：['mɑːkit'pleis] *n.* 市场
[3] **orders**：*n.* 订单
[4] **minimum**：['miniməm] *adj.* 最小的
[5] **escrow**：['eskrəu] *n.* 国际支付宝
[6] **delivery**：[di'livəri] *n.* 交货
[7] **tracking**：['trækiŋ] *n.* 追踪
[8] **one-stop-shop**：*n.* 一站式商店

The **steps** for doing business in Aliexpress are as following:

(1) buyer searches products.

(2) buyer orders on line.

(3) buyer payment **secured**.

(4) supplier ships order.

(5) buyer **confirms** delivery.

(6) supplier receives payment.

While doing business through Aliexpress, you will use Escrow service very often.

The Escrow service on Aliexpress is **powered** by

[9] **steps**：*n.* 步骤

[10] **secured**：[si'kjuə] *adj.* 被保障

[11] **confirms**：confirm [kən'fəːm] 的第三人称单数形式，*v.* 确认

[12] **powered**：power ['pauə] 的过去分词形式，*v.* 被推动

Alipay.com, a leading **third-party** online payment platform from the Alibaba Group. Escrow allows you to pay securely online without exposing your credit card details. You can also track delivery of your order and payment is only **released** to the supplier after you confirm you've received the order. Escrow is fast, safe and easy to use!

For Buyers:

Payment will only be released to the supplier after you confirm you've received the order.

Track delivery using a **unique** tracking number on the shipping company's website.

For Suppliers:

Escrow **verifies** the credit card details for every **transaction**.

Escrow only asks you to ship the order after we confirm payment is received.

Launched in 2004, **Alipay** (www.alipay.com) is a **commonly used** third-party online payment solution in China. Alipay provides an escrow payment service that **reduces transaction risk** for online consumers. Shoppers have the ability to verify whether they are happy with goods before releasing funds to the seller. On November 11, 2013, Alipay **set a record** for the highest daily number of transactions, processing **188 million payments** during a 24-hour period. 45.18 million of those transactions, with a total transaction volume of **RMB11.3 billion**, were **facilitated** by **mobile devices**.

---

[1] **third-party**: n. 第三方

[2] **released**: v. 放款

[3] **unique**: [juːˈniːk] adj. 独一无二的

[4] **verifies**: verify [ˈverifai] 的第三人称单数形式, v. 核实

[5] **transaction**: n. 交易

[6] **Alipay**: n. 支付宝

[7] **commonly used**: 普遍使用的

[8] **reduces**: reduce [riˈdjuːs] 的第三人称单数形式, v. 减少

[9] **transaction risk**: 交易风险

[10] **set a record**: 创造纪录

[11] **188 million payments**: 1.88 亿笔支付

[12] **RMB11.3 billion**: 113 亿人民币

[13] **facilitated**: facilitate [fəˈsiliteit] 的过去分词形式, v. 促进

[14] **mobile devices**: 移动设备

Alipay continues to **extend** its leadership in online payments to merchants outside of the Alibaba and Taobao marketplaces, with more than 460,000 **external** merchants using Alipay as their **preferred** online payment platform, including leading **local brands** Lenovo, CCTV, Aigo, and New Oriental.

Alipay's products and services are built on trust. Not only does Alipay guarantee the safety of each online transaction, it helps Internet users create their own trust **profile** which **fosters** a safe online payment environment.

To provide Alipay, Alibaba has **partnered** with all the leading banks in China, including Bank of China, China Construction Bank, Agricultural Bank of China, and the Industrial and Commercial Bank of China, as well as **visa** and other **financial institutions**. Alipay has received the **endorsement** of traditional banks and financial institutions because of its **advanced** E-commerce payment technology and **sophisticated** risk management system. Alipay wants to be the E-commerce payment partner of choice for financial institutions.

[1] **extend**：[iks'tend] *v.* 扩展
[2] **external**：[eks'tə:nl] *adj.* 外部的
[3] **preferred**：[pri'fə:d] *adj.* 首选的
[4] **local brands**：本土品牌
[5] **profile**：['prəufail] *n.* 简介
[6] **fosters**：foster ['fɔstə] 的第三人称单数形式，*v.* 培育
[7] **partnered**：partner ['pɑ:tnə] 的过去分词形式，*v.* 与……合作
[8] **visa**：*n.* 维萨（一信用卡组织）
[9] **financial institutions**：*n.* 金融机构
[10] **endorsement**：[in'dɔ:smənt] *n.* 支持
[11] **advanced**：[əd'vɑ:nst] *adj.* 领先的
[12] **sophisticated**：[sə'fistikeitid] *adj.* 精密的

# Exercise 4:

Choose the best option and fill in the bracket with the mark No..

1. The spacecraft will send back (　　) on surface wind and temperatures.

   A. many new informations  　　　　B. a new information

   C. some new information  　　　　D. a few new information

2. My dentist appointment is on Friday, (　　).

   A. fifth October  　　　　B. five October

   C. the fifth of October  　　　　D. the five of October

3. They got there (　　) we by 20 minutes.

   A. more early as  　　　　B. earlier than

   C. as early as  　　　　D. more earlier than

4. The food that Mark is cooking in the kitchen (　　) delicious.

   A. smells  　　　　B. is smelling

   C. has smelled  　　　　D. has been smelling

5. The radio (　　) by my son just now.

   A. has been repaired  　　　　B. is being repaired

   C. repaired  　　　　D. has repaired

6. (　　) pure lead, the lead ore is mined, then smelted, and finally refined.

   A. Obtaining  　　　　B. Being obtained

   C. To obtain  　　　　D. It is obtained

7. I was ill that day. Otherwise I (　　) part in the parade.

   A. would take  　　　　B. would have taken

   C. took  　　　　D. had taken

8. Get me a hammer from the kitchen, (　　)?

   A. will you  　　B. would you  　　C. shall you  　　D. do you

9. The girl (　　) work won the prize is the youngest in her class.

   A. who  　　B. whose  　　C. that  　　D. for whom

10. (　　) and to go skiing are popular winter sports in the northern United States.

    A. Ice-skating  　　　　B. Ice-skate

    C. To go ice-skating  　　　　D. Going ice-skating

参考译文及答案

# 单元八　贸易术语

博客

### 价格术语

在我的网店获得一点成功之后，我听说有些人已经开始在互联网上通过一些平台做国际贸易，比如阿里巴巴、环球资源等。在金融危机之后，越来越多的买家在下订单给卖家时变得谨慎，他们的下单变成了少数量、多次数的形式。

与此同时，阿里巴巴发现了这样的趋势，相应地推出了阿里速卖通。阿里速卖通是提供给卖家直接销售给国际买家的平台，与淘宝类似，但是是针对国际贸易而非国内贸易。

我对将我的商品通过快递卖给国外买家很感兴趣，但是在报价之前必须先懂得价格术语。因为国际贸易中的报价与国内贸易完全不同。

我记得在课堂上学过一些价格术语。FOB、CFR 和 CIF 是 3 个在国际贸易中最频繁使用的基本价格术语。掌握这些价格是起步所必需的。

FOB 的意思是"放在甲板即自由"，它的含义是这个价格包括卖家将货物运至装货港转载工具的甲板上为止的所有费用及利润。

CFR 的意思是"成本加运费"，它的含义是这个价格包括卖家将货物装在转载工具上运至卸货港为止的所有费用及利润。

CIF 的意思是"成本、运费加保险"，它的含义是这个价格包括卖家将货物装在转载工具上运至卸货港为止的所有费用、利润及保险费。

主要的运输方式有卡车、火车、轮船、飞机和管道。运费相差很大，最终将影响价格。电子商务国际贸易的主要运输方式是通过快递。当然无论卖家采用何种运输方式，运费都将加入价格由买方负担。

国际贸易中的保险通常分为 3 种，即平安险、水渍险和一切险。

平安险的含义是单独海损不赔，水渍险的含义是单独海损也赔，一切险的含义是一般一切外来风险都赔。投保平安险的费率大约是 CIF 价格的 110%的 3‰，水渍险的费率大约是 4‰，一切险的费率则大约是 5‰。这外加的 10%是作为买家的预期利润的。最普遍的投保方法是由卖家支付 CIF 价格的 110%的 5‰来投保一切险，并将保费加入价格。

因此，CIF 价格高于 CFR 价格，CFR 价格高于 FOB 价格。

精读

### 为什么国际贸易中的价格相差这么大？

在国际贸易中，价格与国内贸易完全不同。FOB、CFR 和 CIF 是 3 种最普遍的价格术语。我们想知道为什么它们相差这么大？为了找到上述 3 个价格的不同之处，我们必须分析它们的构成。

FOB=采购成本(或制造费用)+国内费用+净利润。采购成本是对贸易商而言，而制造费用是对生产商而言，净利润是对两者而言。

CFR=采购成本（或制造费用）+国内费用+国外运费+净利润。在这个价格术语中，卖方需要为货物运输支付国外运费并将成本加入最终的价格。它意味着 CFR 价格通常要比 FOB 价格高，因为 CFR 价格包括了国外运费而 FOB 价格并不包括。

CIF=采购成本（或制造费用）+国内费用+国外运费+国外保险费+净利润+国外运费。它意味着 CIF 价格比 CFR 价格高，因为卖家在 CIF 价格术语下需要支付国外保险费而在 CFR 价格条款下他们不需要支付这项费用。

因此，CIF 价格在这 3 项价格位列最高，CFR 价格居次，FOB 价格最低。

泛读

## 保险

保险是为了阻止某些不确定和不可预知的风险。需要保险服务的一方称为"被保险人"，而提供保险服务的一方被称为"保险人"。比如，如果发货人将货物发给收获人，收获人要求发货人投保，投保的那一方将会被保险，而保险公司即是保险人。

保险人将会根据被保险人所投保的险别负责某些赔偿。风险分成两类：海上风险和外来风险。

海上风险包括自然灾害和意外事故。自然灾害在此表示一些人力不可抗拒的灾难，比如恶劣天气、雷电、海啸、地震和火山爆发等。意外事故在此是指偶然且不可预料的事故，比如搁浅、触礁、沉没、碰撞、失踪、失火和爆炸等。这些外来风险又分成两类：一般外来风险和特殊外来风险。一般外来风险包括偷窃、短量、沾污、泄漏、破碎、受热受潮、串味、生锈、钩损、淡水雨淋、短少和提货不着和破损等。特殊外来风险包括战争、罢工及政策等。

损失也分成两类：全部损失和部分损失。在全部损失中，又分成实际全损和推定全损。在部分损失中，又分成共同海损和单独海损。

平安险只为共同海损负责；水渍险只为共同海损和单独海损负责；一切险为共同海损、单独海损和一般外来风险负责。尽管它的名字叫一切险，但是它实际上并不为一切风险负责。

相关链接

### 阿里速卖通、国际支付宝和阿里支付宝

（来源：http://help.aliexpress.com/newuserguide；
http://escrow.aliexpress.com/escrow-features/what-is-escrow.html；
https://www.alipay.com/static/aboutalipay/englishabout.htm）

阿里速卖通是由阿里巴巴提供的连最小订单都可以享受批发价格的新的批发市场。即使少到 1 件商品，也可获得国际支付宝保障和快递交货全程追踪，阿里速卖通是您真正的一站式商店！

在阿里速卖通做生意的步骤如下。

(1) 买家搜索货物。
(2) 买家在线下单。
(3) 买家国际支付宝保障。
(4) 卖家发货。
(5) 买家确认收货。

（6）卖家收到货款。

在阿里速卖通做生意，你还将经常使用国际支付宝服务。

速卖通上的国际支付宝服务由阿里支付宝推动，是来自阿里巴巴集团的领先的在线第三方支付平台。国际支付宝允许你不用泄露信用卡细节实现在线安全支付。你也可以追踪你的订单交货，付款只有在你确认收到所订购的货物时才会放款给卖家。国际支付宝使用迅速、安全且容易！

对买家而言：

付款只有在你确认收到所订购的货物时才会放款给卖家。

使用唯一追踪号在运输公司网站上追踪交货。

对卖家而言：

国际支付宝为每一次交易核实信用卡。

国际支付宝只会在确认收到付款后才要求你发货。

支付宝自2004年推出后已成为中国普遍使用的第三方在线支付解决方案。阿里支付宝提供第三方支付担保服务为在线消费者减少了交易风险。买家可以在放款给卖家之前核实他们是否喜欢所购商品。在2013年11月11日（双十一），阿里支付宝创造了日交易额的最高纪录，在24小时内处理了1.88亿笔交易。其中的4518万笔交易、高达113亿元人民币的交易额，是通过移动设备实现的。

阿里支付宝在阿里巴巴和淘宝市场之外持续扩大其对商家的影响力，超过46万外部商家使用阿里支付宝作为其首选的在线支付平台，包括国内著名的品牌：联想、中央电视台、爱国者和新东方。

阿里支付宝的产品和服务都是基于信任。阿里支付宝不仅可以保障每笔在线交易的安全性，它也希望帮助互联网用户创建自己的简介，来培育安全的在线支付环境。

为了推广阿里支付宝，阿里巴巴与所有中国的领先银行合作，包括中国银行、中国建设银行、中国农业银行和中国工商银行，以及维萨和其他国际金融机构。阿里支付宝已经由于其先进的电子商务支付技术和精密的风险管理系统得到了传统银行和金融机构的支持。阿里支付宝想要成为金融机构在电子商务支付中的可信赖的合作伙伴。

练习一　（略）

练习二　（见附录二）

练习三　（略）

练习四　1. C　2. C　3. B　4. A　5. A　6. C　7. B　8. A　9. B　10. C

# Unit Nine
## Global Trading

Blog: My Global Trading

Intensive Reading: Exploring Distribution Channel Online

Extensive Reading: China's E-Commerce Companies Go Global

Related Links: Alibaba.com

## My Global Trading

It's just another **weekend** and it's odd that I was asked to come back home. I'm happy about this although I'm not sure what happened. Normally, I spend weekends in school as my parents are always very busy. I would like to share weekend with them. As soon as I arrived home this afternoon, mom and dad were waiting for me and seemed **excited**. Didn't allow me to sit down, mom dragged me to the study room and released me **in front of** the computer.

It's web page of **Alibaba.com** in front of me. Be aware of my doubt, mom smiled and told me the story. My parents company had just registered with Alibaba.com for **export** purpose a week ago and had one order come few days ago. Mom said she was so happy to have this result but was confused about the follow up job.

I remember mom had been **complaining** about the sales **decline** of the business. My parents operate a small

[1] **weekend**：[wiːkˈend] n. 周末

[2] **excited**：[ikˈsaitid] adj. 激动的，兴奋的，活跃的

[3] **in front of**：在……前面

[4] **Alibaba.com**：阿里巴巴网站

[5] **export**：[ˈekspɔːt] n. 输出，出口

[6] **complaining**：complain [kəmˈplein] 的 ing 形式，v. 控诉，抱怨

[7] **decline**：[diˈklain] n. 衰退

[1] **toy factory**：玩具厂
[2] **domestic**：[də'mestik] *adj.* 国内的
[3] **international**：[,intə(:)'næʃənəl] *adj.* 国际的
[4] **trade agents**：外贸代理
[5] **financial crisis**：金融危机
[6] **encountered**：encounter [in'kauntə] 的过去式，*v.* 遭遇
[7] **sales volume**：销售量
[8] **staff**：[stɑ:f] *n.* 员工
[9] **operating costs**：营业成本
[10] **turned around**：转机
[11] **industry meeting**：行业会议
[12] **sales channel**：销售渠道
[13] **enquiries**：enquiry [in'kwairi] 的复数，*n.* （贸易）询盘
[14] **simulation operation**：模拟操作
[15] **subsidiaries**：subsidiary [səb'sidjəri] 的复数，*n.* 子公司
[16] **marketplaces**：市场
[17] **third-party online payment systems**：第三方在线支付系统

**toy factory** for over five years. These toys are sold to both **domestic** and **international** markets. The factory has **trade agents** dealing with the orders. Since the breaking of the global **financial crisis**, many Chinese manufacturing companies **encountered** a decline of orders and **sales volu- me**, just like my parents. The factory had to reduce **staff** to keep the **operating costs** low.

Things **turned around** last week when mom attended an **industry meeting**, and was introduced to use the online trading platform to extend **sales channel**. My parents chose Alibaba as a try. They registered with the free service and uploaded some information about the factory and the products. To their surprise, customers' **enquiries** came so- on and one order was completed yesterday.

Mom said she never expected the internet could bring orders to the business. And now she faces an issue to find a person to operate the online business. Then, she thought of me.

We had learnt about the story of Alibaba Group in class and did **simulation operation** about online platforms of Alibaba Group. I shortly explained the services to mom and dad. Alibaba Group owns several **subsidiaries** including many aspects about E-business such as B2B/B2C/C2C online **marketplaces**, **third-party online payment systems**, search engines, etc.. It works as third-party trade platform for buyers and sellers and has already become the leading brand in internet world.

Alibaba.com is one of the subsidiaries of Alibaba Group and operates three online trade marketplaces to enable buyers and sellers around the world trading together. It can help **manufacturers**, exporters and companies planning to export, to market themselves cost-effectively on a global scale by providing **qualified** foreign buyers with information about their products and services.

Since our toys are mainly sold to **European** and **North America** markets, my parents registered with the global trade marketplace (www.alibaba.com) as a toy exporter.

Alibaba.com offers different level of functions for paid and unpaid users. For example, if members **update** to **China Gold Supplier**, they have to pay RMB29,800 to get **membership** with pretty more functions and services. Apart from membership fees, some extra **transaction fees** are charged when orders are successfully finished through the platform.

[1] **manufacturers**: manufacturer [ˌmænjuˈfæktʃərə] 的复数, n. 制造商，厂商

[2] **qualified**: [ˈkwɔlifaid] adj. 有资格的

[3] **European**: [ˌjuərəˈpi(ː)ən] adj. 欧洲的

[4] **North America**: 北美

[5] **update**: [ʌpˈdeit] v. 更新

[6] **China Gold Supplier**: 中国供应商

[7] **membership**: [ˈmembəʃip] n. 会员身份

[8] **transaction fees**: 交易费

[1] **Aliexpress**：全球速卖通
[2] **wholesale**：['həulseil] *n.* 批发
[3] **registration**: [,redʒis'treiʃən] *n.* 登记，注册
[4] **foreign markets**：国外市场
[5] **express delivery**：快递
[6] **offline**：线下的
[7] **optimize**: ['ɔptimaiz] *v.* 使最优化
[8] **affilate marketing**：联盟营销，会员制营销
[9] **permission marketing**：许可营销
[10] **commission**: [kə'miʃən] *n.* 佣金

A new function was released in the global platform called **Aliexpress**. This is a new service focusing on **wholesale** market online and was only available free for China Gold Supplier when it was released. Now this service is free and is open for **registration**. Small business can do wholesale business here. The buyers on this platform would be small buyers from the **foreign markets**. The amount of the order can be as low as one item with international **express delivery** required. Thus, our products are selling to not only foreign import companies, but also retailers both online or **offline**.

To be a successful seller on this platform, E-marketing is required to **optimize** the information to get more potential customers. The main tools are SEO, PPC, **affilate marketing**, **permission marketing**, etc..

To increase the orders, my parents are happy to pay membership fees and have **commission** charged. From now on, I'll in charge of this international trading channel for my parents. I believe I can use my knowledge to bring profit to our factory.

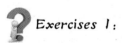
Exercises 1：

Speaking: Discuss the topic of international trade online and give your own understanding in English (50~100 words).

Writing: Write down your understanding about the benefits to use internet doing international trade (not less than 100 words).

## Notes

(1) weekend 指的是周六和周日。周一到周五称为 weekday。

(2) excited 兴奋的，激动的。形容词形式是 exciting，名词形式是 excitement。

(3) in front of 在……前面，与 in back of(在……后面)对应。

(4) Alibaba.com 阿里巴巴旗下的三大贸易平台之一，国际贸易平台。中文平台是 china.alibaba.com，日文平台是 alibaba.com.jp。

(5) export 出口，与 import(进口)相对应。exporter 表示出口商，出口公司，出口国。

(6) decline 消减，下降。on the decline 在消减。也作动词，下降。也可理解为拒绝，谢绝。

(7) domestic and international markets 国内和国际市场。国内也可用 national 表示。国外市场也可用 foreign，指本国以外的。

(8) trade agent 外贸代理。在工厂和国外进口商之间存在的一种角色，通常很多工厂没有自营进出口权，便由具备资质的外贸中介如外贸公司，来办理出口相关手续；也可以是外贸中介/公司在接到订单后，从工厂购货。

(9) financial crisis 金融危机。最近的一次金融危机是 2008 年爆发的，由美国房地产泡沫引发的世界级的金融危机。金融危机对出口的影响是，美元贬值、我国产品出口优势减少，从而导致出口市场的整体下滑。

(10) staff 职员，员工。相当于 employees，经常用于代表全体工作人员，如 the hotel staff 旅馆全体工作人员。另有非常类似的词语 stuff，是材料、东西的意思，容易混淆。

(11) turn around　显示相反的，这里译为出现转机。

(12) 国际贸易中，询价用 enquiry 表示，报价用 quotation 表示。

(13) Alibaba Group　阿里巴巴集团，旗下有多个子公司，包括阿里巴巴网络有限公司、淘宝网、支付宝、阿里巴巴云计算、中国雅虎等。

(14) simulation operation　模拟操作。simulation 是模拟的意思，尤用于软件系统、新型技术等的模拟运行。

(15) subsidiary　子公司。可用 subcompany 来表示下属公司，母公司用 parent company 或 holding company 来表示。

(16) third-party online payment system　第三方在线支付系统，为网络贸易提供交易平台，如支付宝、快钱、PayPal 等。

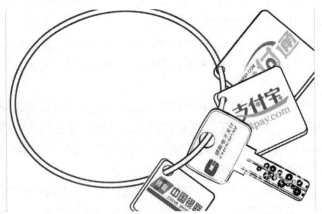

(17) manufacturer　厂商，制造商。厂商生产的产品叫做 manufactures，也可用 product、output、finished goods 来表示生产出来的产品。而工厂用 factory 表示，供应商用 supplier 表示。

(18) qualified　有资格的。企业出口要具备的自营进出口权，就是企业能否做进出口的一种资格。具备进出口权的企业在出口时可以称为 qualified companies。在网络贸易平台上，如阿里巴巴国际贸易平台在审核买方信息后，进行发布，这些国际买家称之为 qualified buyers，来体现买家的可靠性。

(19) Europe and North America markets　欧美市场。欧洲市场上由 20 多个国家结成的联盟，称为 European Union，简称 EU（欧盟），是欧洲市场向世界其他国家进出口的一个联合体，中国很多外贸企业与欧洲国家有贸易摩擦时，都是与欧盟进行商讨的。

(20) update　更新，也作名词形式。产品的更新换代，软件的更新，信息的更新都可以用这个词，如 update to the newest version、updated news。

(21) China Gold Supplier  中国供应商。阿里巴巴向中国出口型企业提供的针对国外市场的 B2B 营销产品的名称，针对的客户群体就是合法注册的中国出口型中小企业，借助互联网寻求商机把产品卖出去。

(22) membership  会员身份。member 也是会员的意思，membership 特指会员资质。

(23) transaction fee  交易费。买家或卖家在交易过程中因接受第三方的服务而产生的费用，在网络贸易中一般由卖家承担交易费用。如 eBay 网上产品陈列费，使用 PayPal 支付工具产生的交易费等。而平台从交易成功后提取一定比例的佣金，可用 commision 来表示。

(24) Aliexpress  全球速卖通，是阿里巴巴 2009 年下半年推出的，是阿里巴巴帮助中小企业接触终端批发零售商，小批量多批次快速销售，拓展利润空间而全力打造的融合订单、支付、物流于一体的外贸在线交易平台。

(25) wholesale  批发。wholesaler 批发商。对应的是 retail 零售，retailer 零售商。

(26) foreign markets  国外市场。通指本国以外的市场。

(27) express delivery  快递。如圆通快递、天天快递等，国际快递有 DHL、UPS、FedEx 等。

(28) offline  线下的，脱机的，离线的，与 online 相对应。这里是对应于网络零售商而言的线下实体零售商。

(29) affiliate marketing  联盟营销，通常是指网络联盟营销，也称联属网络营销、会员制营销，是一种按营销效果付费的网络营销方式，即商家(又称广告主，在网上销售或宣传自己产品和服务的厂商)利用专业联盟营销机构(百通等联盟平台)提供的网站联盟服务拓展其线上及线下业务，扩大销售空间和销售渠道，并按照营销实际效果支付费用的新型网络营销模式。最早由 Amazon.com 推出会员制营销。

(30) permission marketing  许可营销。基于因特网的发展而出现的一种较新的营销概念。企业在推广其产品或服务的时候，事先征得顾客的"许可"。得到潜在顾客许可之后，通过 E-mail 的方式向顾客发送产品/服务信息，因此，许可营销也就是许可 E-mail 营销。

## Tips for Translation

(1) 在翻译中英文时，要懂得如何选择恰当的词汇。比如：domestic 和 national、foreign 和 international。foreign 指的是本国以外的市场，international 通指国际市场，也包含本国。而 domestic 和 national 都是国内的意思。

(2) sales 这个词来自于 sell，可作名词销售量，也可作形容词销售的。因而，后面可以跟很多与销售相关的名词，在翻译销售平台、销售渠道、销量、销售数据等，都可以用，如 sales platform、sales channel、sales volume、sales figure。

(3) 翻译一些新生的专有词汇时，如 China Gold Supplier、Aliexpress，这些都是阿里巴巴国际贸易平台推出的产品，应该根据官方的中文命名，而不是单纯地根据它的字面翻译，这两个词的中文命名为中国供应商，全球速卖通。

(4) 在网上交易过程中，经常会出现的两个词：transaction fee 和 commission，即交易费和佣金。在理解的时候，佣金是交易成功后，作为中介方收取的费用，而交易费是在以交易为目的的贸易过程中产生的相关费用。在很多情况下，交易没有达成，交易费也是要收取的，比如说商品陈列费。

(5) 网络营销中会出现一些新词汇，其中一些是基于以前的基础发展起来的，在翻译和理解的时候应该多参考资料。如 affiliate marketing 翻译为联盟营销、联属营销等，在中国台湾地区也有翻译为伙伴行销，它是在 Amazon.com 推出的会员制营销的基础上发展起来的，应根据英文原称来查找分析它的意思。

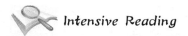 Intensive Reading

## Exploring Distribution Channel Online

E-business has broken the **geographical restriction** and brought great **business opportunities** for the world economy. As the growing of E-business, companies has become aware of the enormous web economy and started to explore global market through the internet. Not only those **multi-national companies**, but the **small and medium enterprises**, are sharing the same global market to sell their products.

The establishment of **ChemNet.com** in 1995 indicates the **emergence** of B2B platform in China which firstly brought Chinese traditional business into internet. From then, B2B platforms **spring up** one after another. Online platforms such as Alibaba.com, **Globalsources.com**, and **Madeinchina.com** are top platforms to provide access to international trade for small and medium enterprises in China. These platforms open a window for Chinese suppliers to attract global buyers.

Be able to provide **trustworthy** and effective services for **purchasers** and manufacturers, B2B platforms have **convinced** traditional small and medium enterprises with this new way to explore the global distribution channel. Some platforms even provide **integrated** all-dimensional trading services, such as on-line and off-line supplier recommendations, **representation** at international shows and trade leads match service, etc.. Both Chinese manufacturers and international purchasers feel confident about each transaction.

[1] geographical restriction：地域限制
[2] business opportunities：商业机会

[3] multi-national companies：跨国公司
[4] small and medium enterprises：中小型企业

[5] ChemNet.com：中国化工网
[6] emergence：[iˈməːdʒəns] n. 出现

[7] spring up：涌现
[8] Globalsources.com：环球资源网
[9] Madeinchina.com：中国制造网

[10] trustworthy：[ˈtrʌstˌwəːði] adj. 可靠的
[11] purchasers：买方
[12] convinced：convince [kənˈvins] 的过去分词形式，v. 使确信

[13] integrated：[ˈintigreitid] adj. 完整的，综合的
[14] representation：[ˌreprizenˈteiʃən] n. 出现，展示

Apart from companies, individuals have also seen opportunities to sell products globally. **Individual sellers** on Taobao.com have started selling products to **oversea buyers**, as well as eBay.cn. And many of those B2B platforms have released wholesale platform for those individual sellers or small global purchasers.

The **prosperity** of E-business has brought huge **benefits** to traditional business. No matter what scale your company is, you are sharing the same global market with others. Meanwhile, the competition will become even **fiercer**. And the eventually **beneficiary** is the consumer.

[1] **Individual sellers**：个人卖家

[2] **oversea buyers**：海外买家

[3] **prosperity**：[prɔs'periti] n. 繁荣，成功

[4] **benefits**：benefit ['benifit] 的复数，n. 利益

[5] **fiercer**：更激烈

[6] **beneficiary**：[beni'fiʃəri] n. 受益人

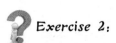

Exercise 2:

List at least two international trading platforms and give comparison.

## Notes

(1) geographical restriction　地域限制。这个词是经常拿来描述电子商务与传统商务的区别，也就是电子商务打破了地域上的限制。也可称作 geographical boundary。

(2) multi-national company　跨国公司。根据地域性和经营性质等，企业有多种称呼，如：local company 本土公司，state-owned enterprise 国有企业，private company 私营企业。

(3) small and medium enterprises　中小企业。这是针对不同行业的不同特点，以职工人数、销售额、资产总额作为划分标准。中小型企业在我国企业中占了大多数，阿里巴巴贸易平台的主营客户群也是中小企业。

(4) ChemNet.com, Globalsources.com, Madeinchina.com 这几个是国内比较知名的贸易平台，分别是中国化工网、环球资源网、中国制造网，与阿里巴巴都存在一定的竞争关系。

(5) trustworthy　可靠的，可信的。这是一个组合词，trust 是信任的意思，worthy 是值得的意思。其他的组合词有 moneybox、eyedropper、mailbox 等。

(6) purchaser　买家，采购商。同 buyer。在企业，采购部门称为 purchasing department。

(7) integrated　集成的，综合的。集成化概念的不断提出，使得这个词的使用率也越来越高，如 integrated marketing 整合营销。名词形式是 integration。

(8) representation　展现，展示。这里作在展会上展示的意思。

(9) individual seller　个人卖家。这里指网上开店的个人卖家。

(10) oversea buyers　海外买家，同 foreign buyers。

(11) benefit　利益。也作动词，使……受益。beneficiary 受益人。

(12) fierce　激烈的。这里用来表示竞争的激烈性，同 severe、intense、rough 等。

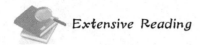
### Extensive Reading

## China's E-Commerce Companies Go Global

Today, China's e-tailers are **embracing** change like never before. **McKinsey & Company** predicts that by 2020 China's e-commerce market will equal that of the US, Japan, the UK, Germany and France combined today. To stay **competitive** in such a huge market these companies need to be **nimble**. For many, internationallization will help strengthen their brand and create new value.

Entrepreneurial Chinese have long sold abroad, on platforms such as eBay Inc. Now, big players are testing the waters. Still, big Chinese firms so far pose little threat to giant U.S. internet retailers such as Amazon.com. But they could offer options to consumers shopping for products in **niche market**. **LightInTheBox** Holdings, for example, started with **wedding gowns** and broadened its offerings to include items such as faucets with lights that change color with the water temperature.

At **Aliexpress**, hair extensions and wigs accounted for 68% of all product purchases in the beauty and health category in the first half of 2013. Buyers in the U.S. accounted for 75% of those purchases, the company said. Most searches in the category are for "**virgin hair**", according to Alibaba. Virgin hair is unprocessed and hasn't been dyed, bleached or permed.

**Vipshop** Holdings Ltd., an online discounter of branded products, is launching a platform for Hong Kong and Macau this month.

[1] **embracing:** embrace [im'breis] 的 ing 形式，v. 迎接
[2] **McKinsey & Company：** 麦肯锡公司

[3] **competitive：** 有竞争力的
[4] **nimble：** 灵活的

[5] **niche market：** 利基市场
[6] **LightInTheBox：** 兰亭集势
[7] **wedding gowns：** 婚纱礼服

[8] **Aliexpress：** 速卖通

[9] **virgin hair：** 原发

[10] **Vipshop：** 唯品会

**VANCL** and **Jingdong** have hundreds of millions of active users but they are by no means global giants yet. Venturing abroad will boost their reputation and help balance the already squeezed profit margins in the increasingly overcrowded home market.

ASOS, the popular UK-headquartered fashion e-tailer recently announced ambitious plans of launching a Chinese website in October. ASOS was following in the footsteps of other companies like online luxury fashion outlet Net-a-Porter that entered China a few months ago.

If Chinese online retailers are serious about taking on global companies such as Amazon.com and eBay, they need to build their own **logistics centers** abroad for more efficient handling. But Chinese companies will only be able to compete globally if they offer global consumers unique value proposition. To achieve that and to move up the value chain, they will need to invest in brand-building. Now, more and more Chinese E-commerce companies are building logistics centers globally to serve the customers worldwide.

[1] **VANCL**：凡客成品
[2] **Jingdong**：京东商城

[3] **logistics centers**：物流中心

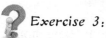 Exercise 3:

1. Talk about the e-tailing sites mentioned in the article in English.
2. Find a case of Chinese company making efforts to the global trade online.

 **Related Links**

## Alibaba.com

(Source: http://news.alibaba.com)

[1] **Company Overview**：企业简介

[2] **flagship**：['flægʃip] n. 旗舰

[3] **millions of**：数以百万计

[4] **importers**：importer [im'pɔ:tə] 的复数，n. 进口商

[5] **exporters**：exporter [iks'pɔ:tə] 的复数，n. 出口商

[6] **associated company**：联营公司

[7] **facilitating**：facilitate [fə,sili'tei] 的 ing 形式，v. 帮助

[8] **community**：[kə'mju:niti] n. 社区

[9] **Alisoft**：阿里软件

[10] **incubates**：incubate [,inkju'beit] 的第三人称单数形式，v. 孵化

[11] **Ali Institute**：阿里学院

[12] **History & Milestones**：历史和里程碑

### Company Overview

Alibaba.com is the global leader in Business- to-Business (B2B) E-commerce and the **flagship** company of Alibaba Group. Founded in 1999, Alibaba.com makes it easy for **millions of** buyers and suppliers around the world to do business online through three marketplaces: a global trade marketplace (www.alibaba.com) for **importers** and **exporters**, a Chinese marketplace (www.alibaba.com.cn) for domestic trade in China, and through an **associated company**, a Japanese marketplace (www.alibaba.co.jp) **facilitating** trade to and from Japan. Together, its marketplaces form a **community** of more than 45 million regis-tered users from more than 240 countries and regions. Alibaba.com also offers business management software solutions targeting small businesses across China under the "**Alisoft**" brand and **incubates** E-commerce talent for small businesses in China through **Ali Institute**. Founded in Hangzhou, China, Alibaba.com has offices in more than 60 cities across Greater China, Japan, Korea, Europe and the United States.

### History & Milestones

Jack Ma, a former English teacher from Hangzhou, started Alibaba.com with 17 other founders in 1999 as a trading platform for small and medium manufacturers to sell their wares.

Since then Alibaba.com has grown into the premier online marketplace for small businesses around the world to identify potential **trading partners** and **interact with** each other to conduct business online. Alibaba.com completed its US$1.7 billion initial public offering on the **Hong Kong Stock Exchange** on November 6th, 2007, the biggest Internet IPO since Google's 2004 offering on the **NASDAQ**.

Some iconic events of the company are listed below:

| | |
|---|---|
| June 1999 | Established Alibaba Group |
| October 2000 | Launched the Gold Supplier membership on the international marketplace to serve exporters in mainland China |
| August 2001 | Launched the International **TrustPass** membership to serve exporters outside mainland China |
| March 2002 | Launched the China TrustPass membership to serve small businesses engaging in domestic China trade |
| July 2002 | Launched **keyword ranking services** on international marketplace |
| November 2003 | Launched the **TradeManager** instant messaging software to enable users to communicate in real time on the marketplaces |
| March 2005 | Launched keyword ranking services on the China marketplace |
| March 2007 | Launched branded advertisements on the China marketplace |
| April 2008 | Launched **Winport** to help small businesses build their own presence on the China marketplace |
| May 2008 | Formed an associated company, Alibaba Japan, with Softbank to take over the operation of our Japanese business |
| June 2008 | Launched the China TrustPass for Individuals membership to serve entrepreneurs engaging in domestic China trade |
| August 2008 | Launched the **Export-to-China** service to help small businesses sell direct to China |
| November 2008 | Launched an entry-level membership package, Gold **Supplier Starter Pack**, on our international marketplace |

[1] **trading partners**：贸易伙伴
[2] **interact with**：与……相互作用

[3] **Hong Kong Stock Exchange**：香港证券交易所（现为香港联交所）

[4] **NASDAQ**：纳斯达克股票交易市场

[5] **TrustPass**：诚信通

[6] **keyword ranking services**：关键字排名服务

[7] **TradeManager**：贸易通

[8] **Winport**：旺铺

[9] **Export-to-China**：出口通

[10] **Supplier Starter Pack**：供应商基础套餐

|  |  |
| --- | --- |
| July 2009 | Launched the Global Gold Supplier membership on our international marketplace to serve suppliers outside of Greater China |
| September 2009 | Beta-launched Aliexpress, a wholesale platform on the international marketplace designed to facilitate small bulk transactions online |

In December 2009, Aliexpress.com was released. This is a new wholesale marketplace from Alibaba.com offering factory prices on even the smallest orders.

What Aliexpress can do?

1. Buy with Confidence from **Verified Suppliers**

Aliexpress is the safest way to buy quality products online. Your payments are fully protected and all suppliers are **authenticated** & verified by a leading inspecttion company. It's safe, fast and simple!

2. **Secure** your Payments with **VeriSign encryption**

Aliexpress Escrow uses industry-leading VeriSign encryption to bring you the most secure transactions online.

3. Browse Thousands of Products at Wholesale Prices

Buy online direct from suppliers to get low wholesale prices on thousands of items. If you're looking for quality, only genuine products are sold on Aliexpress. Buy in small lots or as little as 1 item. It's your choice.

4. Get Express Delivery with **Full Tracking**

All orders on Aliexpress are shipped fast and can be tracked at any stage of delivery using a unique tracking number. With **DHL, UPS, EMS** and other leading **shipping companies** making delivery, your orders are also in very safe hands.

---

[1] **Verified Suppliers**：经验证的供应商

[2] **authenticated**：authenticate [ɔːˈθentikeit] 的过去分词形式，v. 鉴定

[3] **Secure**：[siˈkjuə] v. 保护

[4] **VeriSign encryption**：威瑞信加密服务

[5] **Full Tracking**：全程跟踪

[6] **DHL**：中外运敦豪快递公司

[7] **UPS**：联合包裹

[8] **EMS**：中国邮政快递

[9] **shipping companies**：海运公司

### Exercise 4:

Choose the best option and fill in the bracket.

1. How many subsidiaries Alibaba Group has? (    )

A. 1                B. 3                C. 4                D. 5

2. Normally, the third-party trading platform charges fees from (    ).

A. buyer                    B. seller

C. both of them             D. none

3. Which product is not belong to Alibaba? (    )

A. Alimama                  B. Alibaby

C. Alisoft                  D. Alicloud

4. Who can be qualified to use Aliexpress? (    )

A. Only seller

B. Only China Gold Supplier

C. One buyer

D. Anyone

5. What services should Ali Institute provides to the users? (    )

A. Sell products overseas

B. Find international buyers

C. E-marketing training

D. Business consultation

参考译文及答案

# 单元九　跨国贸易

博客

## 我的跨国贸易

又是一个周末，奇怪的是，家里来电话让我回家。虽然不知道发生了什么事，我还是觉得很高兴。平常因为家里人太忙，周末我都是在学校过的。我总想能够跟他们一起过周末。下午我到家的时候，爸妈已经在等我了，看起来还很高兴。还没来得及坐下，妈妈就拉着我去书房的电脑跟前。

电脑屏幕上是阿里巴巴国际网站的页面。看出我的疑虑，妈妈便笑着开始解释给我听。原来爸妈的公司在一个星期前在阿里巴巴国际网站上注册了出口商，几天前就来了一个订单。妈妈很高兴，但是却不知道接下来怎么做。

我记得最近妈妈都在抱怨生意差了。我的父母经营一家玩具工厂五年了，产品卖往国内外市场。外单一直都是由外贸公司来做。全球金融危机后，很多中国生产企业遇到了订单减少、销量下滑的情况。爸妈的工厂也是，只好通过裁员来降低经营成本。

就在上周，事情有了转机。妈妈去参加了一个行业会议，有人介绍她使用网上平台来扩展销售渠道。于是，他们选择了阿里巴巴，并注册了免费账户，上传了一些产品和工厂的信息。出乎意料，很快便有客户来咨询，到昨天还完成了一笔订单。

妈妈说她没想到网络还能带来订单。现在，她急于要找适合的人来帮忙运作网上生意。于是，就想到我了。

我们在课堂上学过阿里巴巴集团的故事，也进行了网上平台的模拟操作。我把阿里巴巴的情况简单地介绍了一下。这个集团拥有多家子公司，业务覆盖面很广，包括 B2B/B2C/C2C 在线交易市场、第三方支付系统、搜索引擎等。它的第三方平台，在业内占据领先地位。

阿里巴巴网络公司是阿里巴巴集团的下属公司，运营着 3 个贸易平台，为来自世界各地的买家卖家提供贸易平台。它给具备一定资质的海外买家提供产品信息和服务，从而帮助厂商、出口商和公司制定出口计划，进行低成本的国际营销。

厂里的玩具主要销往欧美市场，所以爸妈以出口商身份注册了国际贸易平台(www.alibaba.com)。

阿里巴巴按照是否收费提供不同的功能。比如，普通会员升级为中国供应商，需花费 29 800 元人民币，但是功能和服务要完善得多。除了会员费，阿里巴巴也会收取一定的交易费用。

一项新的国际性服务平台推出了，那就是全球速卖通。这个新的平台主要是针对国际批发的贸易平台，刚出来的时候，只对中国供应商免费使用。现在这个平台已经开放免费注册，小企业也都可以在这里做批发生意，而买家也可能是来自海外的小买家。订单数量可以小到一件物品，并且用国际快递配送。这样，我们的产品不仅仅可以卖给国外进口商，其他线上线下的零售商也都可以了。

想要在阿里巴巴平台上取得成功，还需要进行网络营销来吸引更多的潜在顾客。这里主要是指通过搜索引擎优化、单击付费广告、联盟营销、许可营销等方法。

为了增加订单，爸妈还是乐意支付平台的会员费和佣金的。从现在起，我要为我的父母来操作这个平台了。我相信我可以用我的知识来给工厂带来效益。

精读

## 开辟网络销售渠道

电子商务打破了传统的地域限制，并为世界经济带来了大量的商机。随着电子商务的发展，企业意识到网络经济的快速增长，开始利用网络来开拓国际市场。国内中小企业也能够像跨国企业一样，向国际市场销售产品。

成立于1995年的中国化工网，作为B2B平台的领先者，首先将中国传统企业引向了网络。此后，B2B平台不断涌现。在线交易平台以阿里巴巴、环球资源网和中国制造网等知名网站为代表的平台，能够为中国的中小企业提供国际市场准入。这些平台为中国供应商吸引国际买家打开了一扇窗。

B2B平台能够为买家和厂商提供可靠、高效的服务，中小企业相信这个平台能够成为开辟国际渠道的新方式。一些平台还提供集成化、全方位的贸易服务，如线上或线下的供应商推荐，提供国际展会展览和贸易配对服务等。国内厂商和国际买家都很信任这种交易方式。

除企业外，个人也能够有机会把产品卖到国际上去。淘宝上的卖家现在可以向海外买家出售产品，eBay.cn也是。而一些B2B网站也开始推出针对个人卖家和国际买家的零售平台。

电子商务的繁荣给传统商业带来了巨大的利益。不论你的企业规模多大，你都能够跟其他企业共享全球市场。但是竞争也会更激烈。而最终的受益人，却是消费者。

泛读

## 中国电商企业的全球化道路

当今中国的网络零售业遭遇了前所未有的变革。麦肯锡预测到2020年，中国的电子商务市场相当于今天美、日、英、德和法国市场的总和。在如此巨大的市场上保持竞争力，企业必须保持灵活的机制。对其中一些企业来说，国际化可以强化品牌形象，创造新的价值。

中国的企业早就开始向海外销售产品,比如eBay这样的平台。现在，大企业也正在进行尝试。目前，中国的大企业还尚未对美国的网络零售商如亚马逊造成什么影响，但是他们给消费者提供了利基市场的产品。例如，兰亭集势一开始销售的是婚礼礼服,后来扩展到销售根据水温变换灯光的水龙头。

2013年上半年，速卖通上假发销售占据了美容美体类别68%的销售份额。美国的买家就占了75%。从阿里巴巴的数据来看，这个类别的搜索关键词主要是"原发"，即没有做过染、漂或烫的头发。

唯品会作为在线品牌产品折扣商，这个月面向香港和澳门发布了平台。

凡客诚品和京东商城都拥有数以百万计的活跃用户，但是他们在全球范围内离电商巨头还有一定的距离。投资海外可以迅速提升它们的声望，平衡国内市场被挤压得可怜的利润空间。

英国知名时尚类网站 ASOS 最近宣布，10 月份将推出中文版网站。继在线奢侈品购物网站颇特女士在几个月前进入中国市场后，ASOS 也跟随了它的脚步。

如果中国的网络零售商像亚马逊、eBay 那样认真考虑全球化的问题，它们需要先建立自己的海外物流中心来提高运营效率。只有给全球消费者提供独特的价值主张，中国的企业才可能有竞争力。达到这一目的，它们需要在品牌建设上进行投入。如今，越来越多的中国电商公司为了服务全球顾客正在全球建设物流中心。

相关链接

## Alibaba.com

（来源：http://news.alibaba.com）

**企业简介**

阿里巴巴网络有限公司为全球领先的小企业 B2B 电子商务公司，也是阿里巴巴集团的旗舰业务。阿里巴巴于 1999 年成立，通过旗下 3 个交易市场协助世界各地数以百万计的买家和供应商从事网上生意。3 个网上交易市场包括：集中服务全球进出口商的国际交易市场（www.alibaba.com）、集中国内贸易的中国交易市场（www.alibaba.com.cn），以及透过一家联营公司经营、促进日本外销及内销的日本交易市场（www.alibaba.co.jp）。3 个交易市场形成一个拥有来自 240 多个国家和地区超过 4500 万名注册用户的网上社区。阿里巴巴也通过"阿里软件"品牌向中国各地的小企业提供商务管理软件解决方案，并通过阿里学院为国内中小企业培育电子商务人才。

阿里巴巴创立于中国杭州市，在大中华地区、日本、韩国、欧洲和美国共设有 60 多个办事处。

**历史和里程碑事件**

1999 年，本为英语教师的马云与另外 17 人在中国杭州市创办了阿里巴巴网站，为小型制造商提供了一个销售产品的贸易平台。

其后，阿里巴巴茁壮成长，成为主要的网上交易市场，让全球的小企业透过互联网寻求潜在贸易伙伴，并且彼此沟通和达成交易。阿里巴巴于 2007 年 11 月 6 日在香港联合交易所上市，集资额达 17 亿美元，仅次于 2004 年在美国纳斯达克上市的互联网公司谷歌所创下的首次公开发售纪录。

以下是企业大事记：

| | |
|---|---|
| 1999 年 6 月 | 阿里巴巴集团成立 |
| 2000 年 10 月 | 中国供应商在国际平台上发布，为国内出口商提供服务 |
| 2001 年 8 月 | 为服务海外出口商，发布国际诚信通会员 |
| 2002 年 3 月 | 发布中国诚信通会员来服务国内市场上的小型企业 |
| 2002 年 7 月 | 国际平台关键词排行服务 |
| 2003 年 11 月 | 推出贸易通即时软件来使买卖双方可以实时交谈 |
| 2005 年 3 月 | 在中国市场推出关键字排行服务 |
| 2007 年 3 月 | 在中国市场推出品牌广告 |
| 2008 年 4 月 | 在中国市场推出诚信通旺铺，帮助中小企业建站 |
| 2008 年 5 月 | 由合作公司 Softbank 组建，共同接管阿里巴巴日本站的工作 |

续表

| 2008 年 6 月 | 推出个人诚信通来为国内企业参与国内贸易 |
| --- | --- |
| 2008 年 8 月 | 推出"出口到中国"服务,帮助国外小企业打开中国市场 |
| 2008 年 11 月 | 国际交易市场推出低门槛会员服务——"Gold Supplier 出口通版" |
| 2009 年 7 月 | 国际交易市场推出"国际 Gold Supplier "会员服务,服务大中华地区以外的供应商 |
| 2009 年 9 月 | 全球速卖通试用版在国际平台推出,作为零售平台促进小额批发的销售 |

2009 年 12 月,全球速卖通正式发布。这是阿里巴巴最新发布的零售平台,提供出厂价的小额批发的产品。

全球速卖通可以做什么呢?

1. 放心同认证供应商做生意

通过全球速卖通,你可以以最安全的方式在网上购买到高质量的产品。支付过程是受到保护的,所有的供应商都经过权威机构验定的。它很安全、迅速、简单!

2. 由 VeriSign 公司为你的支付提供保障

全球速卖通的支付担保使用业内领头羊 VeriSign 技术来让你的网上交易更安全。

3. 查阅数千种产品的批发价格

直接通过网络以较低的批发价向供应商购买数千种产品。你可以在这里找到高质量的真品。批量购买或者单件,随你选择。

4. 通过全程跟踪系统来提供快递服务

所有全球速卖通上的订单都会迅速地发出,并且可以通过唯一的查询单号来跟踪货物的走向。通过 DHL、UPS、EMS 这些主流运输公司的配送,你的订单将非常安全。

```
练习一    (略)
练习二    (略)
练习三    (略)
练习四    1. D    2. B    3. D    4. D    5. C
```

# 附录一  电子商务常用术语中英文对照表

| 缩写 | 英语全称 | 中文释义 |
|---|---|---|
| ADSL | Asymmetric Digital Subscriber Line | 非对称数字用户线路 |
| ANSI | American National Standard Institute | 美国国家标准协会 |
| API | Application Program Interface | 应用程序接口 |
| ASP | Active Server Pages | 动态服务器页面 |
| ATM | Asynchronous Transfer Mode | 异步传输模式 |
| ATM | Automatic Teller Machine | 自动柜员机 |
| B2B | Business to Business | 企业对企业的电子商务 |
| B2C | Business to Consumer | 企业对消费者的电子商务 |
| BBS | Bulletin Board System | 电子公告栏，论坛 |
| C2C | Consumer to Consumer | 消费者对消费者的电子商务 |
| CA | Certification Authority | 认证中心 |
| CEO | Chief Executive Officer | 首席执行官 |
| CFO | Chief Financial Officer | 首席财务官 |
| CGI | Common Gateway Interface | 公共网关接口 |
| CIO | Chief Information Officer | 首席信息官 |
| COO | Chief Operation Officer | 首席营运官 |
| CSP | Commerce Service Provider | 商务服务商 |
| CTO | Chief Technology Officer | 首席技术官 |
| DNS | Domain Name Server | 域名服务器 |
| EC | Electronic Commerce | 电子商务 |
| EDI | Electronic Data Interchange | 电子数据交换 |
| EFT | Electronic Funds Transfer | 电子资金转账 |
| E-mail | Electronic Mail | 电子邮件 |
| ERP | Enterprise Resource Planning | 企业资源规划 |
| FTP | File Transfer Protocol | 文件传输协议 |
| GUI | Graphical User Interface | 图形用户界面 |
| HTML | Hyper Text Markup Language | 超文本标识语言 |
| HTTP | Hyper Text Transfer Protocol | 超文本传输协议 |
| IAP | Internet Access Provider | 因特网接入服务商 |

续表

| 缩写 | 英语全称 | 中文释义 |
|---|---|---|
| ICQ | I Seek You | 网络寻呼机 |
| IMAP | Internet Message Access Protocol | 因特网信息访问协议 |
| IP | Internet Protocol | 网际协议（因特网协议） |
| ISP | Internet Service Provider | 因特网服务提供商 |
| LAN | Local Area Network | 局域网 |
| MIME | Multipurpose Internet Mail Extension | 多用因特网邮件扩展 |
| NAP | Network Access Point | 网络访问点 |
| NCP | Network Control Protocol | 网络控制协议 |
| NCSA | National Center for Supercomputing Application | 全美超级计算应用中心 |
| ODBC | Open Data Base Connectivity | 开放数据库连接 |
| ORMS | Operating Resource Management System | 运营资源管理系统 |
| POP3 | Post Office Protocol 3 | 邮局协议 3（一种接收邮件的协议） |
| POTS | Plain Old Telephone Service | 传统的电话服务 |
| SCM | Supply Chain Management | 供应链管理 |
| SET | Secure Electronic Transaction | 安全电子交易 |
| SMTP | Simple Message Transfer Protocol | 简单邮件传送协议（一种发送邮件的协议） |
| TCP | Transmission Control Protocol | 传输控制协议 |
| URL | Uniform Resource Locator | 统一资源定位格式（web 的地址编码） |
| VAN | Value Added Network | 增值网 |
| VPN | Virtual Private Network | 虚拟专用网络 |
| WTO | World Trade Organization | 世界贸易组织 |
| WWW | World Wide Web | 万维网、全球网 |
| XML | Extensible Markup Language | 扩展标记语言 |

# 附录二 全球知名电子商务网站60例

1. ALIBABA http://www.alibaba.com
2. MADE IN CHINA http://www.madeinchina.com
3. GLOBAL SOURCES http://www.globalsources.com
4. TRADE UK http://tradeuk.brightstation.com
5. EC PLAZA http://www.ecplaza.net
6. ECROBOT http://www.ecrobot.com
7. WORLDBIZCLUB http://www.wbc.com
8. WORLD BID http://www.worldbid.com
9. EC21 http://www.ec21.net
10. FOREIGN-TRADE http://www.foreign-trade.com
11. BUSY TRADE http://www.busytrade.com
12. COUNTYWEB http://tradeboard.countyweb.co.uk
13. BS-OFFICE100 http://www.bs-office100.com
14. NETTRADE 21 http://www.nettrade21.net
15. NUDEAL http://www.nudeal.com
16. FREE TRADE FRONT http://www.freetradefront.com
17. BPGTO NETVIGATOR http://bpgto.netvigator.com
18. GO 4 WORLD BUSINESS http://www.go4worldbusiness.com
19. TRADELEAD http://www.tradelead.com
20. EXTREM http://www.extrem.ro
21. ASIA TRADE http://www.asiatrade.com
22. EXPORT http://www.export.com
23. BIDMIX http://www.bidmix.com
24. BIG EXPORT http://www.bigex.com
25. INTL-TRADE http://www.intl-trade.com
26. BEST CLEARANCE http://www.bestclearance.com
27. FIND OFFER http://www.findoffer.com
28. MANUFACTURE http://manufacture.com.tw
29. SWISS INFO http://www.swissinfo.com
30. AA WORLD TRADE http://www.aaworldtrade.com
31. CASANET http://www.casanet.ma
32. CENTRETRADE http://www.centretrade.com
33. GOLDEN-TRADE http://www.golden-trade.com
34. EXTRADE http://www.extrade.net
35. BIZ-CHANNEL http://www.biz-channel.com

36. TRADEZONE http://www.tradezone.com
37. EC TRADE http://www.ectrade.com
38. TRADE ASIA http://www.etradeasia.com
39. CHINA VISTA http://www.chinavista.com
40. SINOSOURCE http://www.sinosource.com
41. ALL PRODUCTS http://www.allproducts.com
42. GLOBAL TRADE WEB http://www.globaltradeweb.com
43. TRADE OFFER http://www.tradeoffer.com
44. TRADE-INDIA http://www.trade-india.com
45. E-WORLD TRADE http://www.e-worldtrade.com
46. EURO PAGES http://www.europages.com
47. MERCOSUR B2B http://www.mercosurb2b.com
48. WORLD CHAMBERS http://www.worldchambers.com
49. PPPINDIA http://www.pppindia.com
50. TRADE EASY http://www.tradeeasy.com
51. FITA http://www.fita.com
52. MEDITERRANEAN TRADE BOARD http://www.eidinet.com
53. B2G PLACE http://www.b2gplace.com
54. YESCO LTD http://www.yescoltd.com
55. WTDB http://www.wtdb.com
56. NET GLOBAL TRADE http://www.netglobaltrade.com
57. TRADE MAMA http://www.trademama.com
58. CLICKIT http://www.clickit.com
59. EC EUROPE http://www.eceurope.com
60. POSTRADE http://www.postrade.com

# 附录三  部分练习答案举例

1. Products

| Kind | From | Logo |
|---|---|---|
| Automobile | from Japan | HONDA |
| TV set | from Japan | SONY |
| Computer | from USA | DELL |
| Shampoo | from USA | P&G |
| Refrigerator | from China | Haier |

2. Brands

| Name | From | Logo |
| --- | --- | --- |
| Coca-Cola | from USA | |
| Mercedes-Benz | from Germany | |
| DANONE | from France | |
| TOYOTA | from Japan | |
| Samsung | from South Korea | |

3. Websites

| Name | Logo |
| --- | --- |
| Baidu | |
| Yahoo! | |
| Sohu | |
| Sina | |

4. E-commerce platforms

| Name | Logo |
|---|---|
| Dangdang | 当当网 dangdang.com |
| Alibaba | 阿里巴巴 1688.com |
| eBay | ebay |
| Taobao | 淘宝网 Taobao.com |

5. Banks

| Name | Logo |
|---|---|
| HSBC(UK) | HSBC |
| Citibank(USA) | citi |

6. Express service providers

| Name | Logo |
|---|---|
| DHL | DHL WORLDWIDE EXPRESS |
| UPS | UPS |
| TNT | TNT |

# 参 考 文 献

[1] 陶树平. 电子商务[M]. 2版. 北京：机械工业出版社，2006.
[2] 徐金宝，解芳. 电子商务概论[M]. 北京：机械工业出版社，2007.
[3] 孙建中. 电子商务专业英语[M]. 2版. 北京：中国水利水电出版社，2006.
[4] 宋梅. 电子商务英语[M]. 北京：科学出版社，2008.
[5] 张云. 电子商务英语[M]. 北京：人民邮电出版社，2005.
[6] 冯英健. 网络营销基础与实践[M]. 北京：清华大学出版社，2007.
[7] Dubosson M., Oserwalder A., Pigneur Y.. *E-business Model Design，Classification and Measurements*[J]. Thunderbird International Business Review, 2002, 44(1):5-23.
[8] Johnson G., Scholes K., Whittington R.. *Exploring Corporate Strategy: Text and Cases*[M]. New Jersey: Prentice Hall, 2005.
[9] Timmers P.. *Business Models for Electronic Markets*[J]. Electronic Markets Journal, 1998, 8(2):7.

# 北京大学出版社第六事业部高职高专营销管理系列教材目录

| 书 名 | 书 号 | 主 编 | 定 价 |
|---|---|---|---|
| ERP沙盘模拟实训教程 | 978-7-301-22697-1 | 钮立新 | 25.00 |
| 连锁经营与管理（第2版） | 即将出版 | 宋之苓 | 35.00（估） |
| 连锁门店管理实务 | 978-7-301-23347-4 | 姜义平，庞德义 | 36.00 |
| 连锁门店开发与设计 | 978-7-301-23770-0 | 马凤棋 | 34.00 |
| 秘书与人力资源管理 | 978-7-301-21298-1 | 肖云林，周君明 | 25.00 |
| 企业管理实务 | 978-7-301-20657-7 | 关善勇 | 28.00 |
| 企业经营ERP沙盘实训教程 | 978-7-301-21723-8 | 葛颖波，张海燕 | 29.00 |
| 企业经营管理模拟训练（含记录手册） | 978-7-301-21033-8 | 叶 萍，宫恩田 | 29.00 |
| 企业行政工作实训 | 978-7-301-23105-0 | 楼淑君 | 32.00 |
| 企业行政管理 | 978-7-301-23056-5 | 张秋垫 | 25.00 |
| 商务沟通实务(第2版) | 978-7-301-25684-8 | 郑兰先，王双萍 | 36.00 |
| 商务礼仪 | 978-7-5655-0176-0 | 金丽娟 | 29.00 |
| 推销与洽谈 | 978-7-301-21278-3 | 岳贤平 | 25.00 |
| 现代企业管理（第2版） | 978-7-301-24054-0 | 刘 磊 | 35.00 |
| 职场沟通实务 | 978-7-301-16175-3 | 吕宏程，程淑华 | 30.00 |
| 中小企业管理（第3版） | 978-7-301-25016-7 | 吕宏程，董仕华 | 38.00 |
| 采购管理实务（第2版） | 978-7-301-17917-8 | 李方峻 | 30.00 |
| 采购实务 | 978-7-301-19314-3 | 罗振华，等 | 33.00 |
| 采购与仓储管理实务 | 978-7-301-23053-4 | 耿 波 | 34.00 |
| 采购与供应管理实务 | 978-7-301-19968-8 | 熊 伟，等 | 36.00 |
| 采购作业与管理实务 | 978-7-301-22035-1 | 李陶然 | 30.00 |
| 仓储管理技术 | 978-7-301-17522-4 | 王 冬 | 26.00 |
| 仓储管理实务（第2版） | 978-7-301-25328-1 | 李怀湘 | 35.00（估） |
| 仓储配送技术与实务 | 978-7-301-22673-5 | 张建奇 | 38.00 |
| 仓储与配送管理（第2版） | 978-7-301-24598-9 | 吉 亮 | 36.00 |
| 仓储与配送管理实务（第2版） | 978-7-301-24597-2 | 李陶然 | 37.00 |
| 仓储与配送管理实训教程（第2版） | 978-7-301-24283-4 | 杨叶勇，姚建凤 | 35.00（估） |
| 仓储与配送管理项目式教程 | 978-7-301-20656-0 | 王 瑜 | 38.00 |
| 第三方物流综合运营（第2版） | 即将出版 | 施学良 | 35.00（估） |
| 电子商务物流基础与实训（第2版） | 978-7-301-24034-2 | 邓之宏 | 33.00 |
| 供应链管理（第2版） | 即将出版 | 李陶然 | 35.00（估） |
| 进出口商品通关 | 978-7-301-23079-4 | 王 巾，佘雪锋 | 25.00 |
| 企业物流管理 | 978-7-81117-804-3 | 傅莉萍 | 32.00 |
| 物流案例与实训（第2版） | 978-7-301-24372-5 | 申纲领 | 35.00 |
| 物流成本管理 | 978-7-301-20880-9 | 傅莉萍，罗春华 | 28.00 |
| 物流经济地理 | 978-7-301-21963-8 | 葛颖波，等 | 29.00 |
| 物流商品养护技术 | 978-7-301-22771-8 | 李燕东 | 25.00 |
| 物流设施与设备 | 978-7-301-22823-4 | 傅莉萍，涂华斌 | 28.00 |
| 物流市场调研 | 978-7-81117-805-0 | 覃 逢，等 | 22.00 |
| 物流市场营销 | 978-7-301-21249-3 | 张 勤 | 36.00 |
| 物流信息技术与应用（第2版） | 978-7-301-24080-9 | 谢金龙，等 | 34.00 |
| 物流信息系统 | 978-7-81117-827-2 | 傅莉萍 | 40.00 |
| 物流信息系统案例与实训 | 978-7-81117-830-2 | 傅莉萍 | 26.00 |
| 物流营销管理 | 978-7-81117-949-1 | 李小叶 | 36.00 |
| 物流运输管理（第2版） | 978-7-301-24971-0 | 申纲领 | 35.00 |
| 物流运输实务（第2版） | 即将出版 | 黄 河 | 35.00（估） |
| 物流专业英语 | 978-7-5655-0210-1 | 仲 颖，等 | 24.00 |
| 现代生产运作管理实务 | 978-7-301-17980-2 | 李陶然 | 39.00 |

| 书 名 | 书 号 | 主 编 | 定 价 |
|---|---|---|---|
| 现代物流概论 | 978-7-81117-803-6 | 傅莉萍 | 40.00 |
| 现代物流管理 | 978-7-301-17374-9 | 申纲领 | 30.00 |
| 现代物流概论 | 978-7-301-20922-6 | 钮立新 | 39.00 |
| 现代物流基础 | 978-7-301-23501-0 | 张建奇 | 32.00 |
| 物流基础理论与技能 | 978-7-301-25697-8 | 周晓利 | 33.00 |
| 新编仓储与配送实务 | 978-7-301-23594-2 | 傅莉萍 | 32.00 |
| 药品物流基础 | 978-7-301-22863-0 | 钟秀英 | 30.00 |
| 运输管理项目式教程（第2版） | 978-7-301-24241-4 | 钮立新 | 32.00 |
| 运输组织与管理项目式教程 | 978-7-301-21946-1 | 苏玲利 | 26.00 |
| 运输管理实务 | 978-7-301-22824-1 | 黄友文 | 32.00 |
| 国际货运代理实务 | 978-7-301-21968-3 | 张建奇 | 38.00 |
| 生产型企业物流运营实务 | 978-7-301-24159-2 | 陈鸿雁 | 38.00 |
| 电子商务实用教程 | 978-7-301-18513-1 | 卢忠敏，胡继承 | 33.00 |
| 电子商务项目式教程 | 978-7-301-20976-9 | 胡 雷 | 25.00 |
| 电子商务英语（第2版） | 978-7-301-24585-9 | 陈晓鸣，叶海鹏 | 27.00 |
| 广告实务 | 978-7-301-21207-3 | 夏美英 | 29.00 |
| 市场调查与统计 | 978-7-301-22890-6 | 陈惠源 | 26.00 |
| 市场调查与预测 | 978-7-301-23505-8 | 王水清 | 34.00 |
| 市场调查与预测 | 978-7-301-19904-6 | 熊衍红 | 31.00 |
| 市场调查与预测情景教程 | 978-7-301-21510-4 | 王生云 | 36.00 |
| 市场营销策划 | 978-7-301-22384-0 | 冯志强 | 36.00 |
| 市场营销理论与实训 | 978-7-5655-0316-0 | 路 娟 | 27.00 |
| 市场营销项目驱动教程 | 978-7-301-20750-5 | 肖 飞 | 34.00 |
| 市场营销学 | 978-7-301-22046-7 | 饶国霞，等 | 33.00 |
| 网络营销理论与实务（第2版） | 即将出版 | 纪幼玲 | 35.00（估） |
| 现代推销技术 | 978-7-301-20088-9 | 尤凤翔，屠立峰 | 32.00 |
| 消费心理与行为分析 | 978-7-301-19887-2 | 王水清，杨 扬 | 30.00 |
| 营销策划（第2版） | 978-7-301-25682-4 | 许建民 | 36.00 |
| 营销策划技术 | 978-7-81117-541-7 | 方志坚 | 26.00 |
| 营销渠道开发与管理 | 978-7-301-21214-1 | 王水清 | 34.00 |

如您需要更多教学资源如电子课件、电子样章、习题答案等，请登录北京大学出版社第六事业部官网www.pup6.cn 搜索下载。

如您需要浏览更多专业教材，请扫下面的二维码，关注北京大学出版社第六事业部官方微信（微信号：pup6book），随时查询专业教材、浏览教材目录、内容简介等信息，并可在线申请纸质样书用于教学。

感谢您使用我们的教材，欢迎您随时与我们联系，我们将及时做好全方位的服务。联系方式：010-62750667，sywat716@126.com，pup_6@163.com，lihu80@163.com，欢迎来电来信。客户服务 QQ 号：1292552107，欢迎随时咨询。